Aristotle Anatomised: The *Poetics* in England 1674-1781

J. C. Eade

Aristotle Anatomised: The *Poetics* in England 1674-1781

Verlag Peter Lang
Frankfurt am Main · Bern · New York · Paris

Library of Congress Cataloging-in-Publication Data

Eade, J. C.:

Aristotle Anatomised: The Poetics in England 1674-1781 /
J. C. Eade. - Frankfurt am Main ; Bern ; New York ; Paris :
Lang, 1988
   ISBN 3-631-40470-0

ISBN 3-631-40470-0
© Verlag Peter Lang GmbH, Frankfurt am Main 1988
All rights reserved.

All parts of this publication are protected by copyright. Any
utilisation outside the strict limits of the copyright law, without
the permission of the publisher, is forbidden and liable to
prosecution. This applies in particular to reproductions,
translations, microfilming, and storage and processing in
electronic retrieval systems.

Printed in Germany

Contents

Introduction	1
Thomas Rymer	7
John Dennis	29
John Dryden	49
Poetic Justice	69
Charles Gildon	79
Joseph Trapp	87
James Harris	101
Select Bibliography	109

INTRODUCTION

This study of the role that Aristotle's *Poetics* played in English neo-classical literary criticism deals with six critics in particular: Thomas Rymer, John Dennis, John Dryden, Charles Gildon, Joseph Trapp, and James Harris. At the end of the seventeenth and at the beginning of the eighteenth century Aristotle had a direct relevance to engaged literary criticism in England. But by the first quarter of the eighteenth century the gentlemen critics were also interpreting him to middle-class audiences. By the last quarter of the century the immediacy had gone.

Since I am concerned with the details of what was done with Aristotle's actual text, I shall take for granted some of the main critical preoccupations of the period (ideas on decorum and the unities, for instance); nor will a comprehensive interpretation of the *Poetics* be offered. Ideally, of course, a study such as the present one, proposing to examine how another age viewed and made use of a particular text, would use a firmly established interpretation of that text as its stable point of reference. But this ideal cannot be realised in the present circumstances, since the *Poetics* still provokes reinterpretation. Furthermore, one major factor in the neo-classical interpretation of the text of the *Poetics* is its complete fragmentation of it. For a number of reasons, then, it is not necessary to adopt a coherent and complete conception of the work.

T.S. Eliot's essay, "The Perfect Critic", gives a warning to those who use Aristotle to explain neo-classical criticism. Eliot says of him that he

> is a person who has suffered from the adherence of persons who must be regarded less as his disciples than his sectaries. One must be firmly distrustful of accepting Aristotle in a canonical spirit; this is to lose the whole living force of him. ... In his short and broken treatise he provides an eternal example ... of intelligence itself swiftly operating the analysis of sensation to the point of principle and definition. It is far less

Aristotle than Horace who has been the model for criticism up to the nineteenth century. A precept, such as Horace, or Boileau gives us, is merely an unfinished analysis ... In matters of great importance the critic must not coerce, and he must not make judgments of worse and better. He must simply elucidate.[1]

To avoid making Aristotle one of his own sectaries I shall make every effort in the following pages to distinguish between intervening commentary and the text of the *Poetics*. I hope in this way to avoid the confusion that Herrick, for instance, could have created when he said of Sir John Harington that he was "closer to the Italian critics, and consequently to Aristotle".[2] Herrick's remark fails to nourish our awareness that, right from the beginning of European commentary on it in late fifteenth-century Italy, the *Poetics* never stood a chance of being interpreted on its own terms. I will say more about this shortly.

There are, I think, three stages necessary in providing a complete picture of the *Poetics* in neo-classical criticism in England. Two of them have already been carried out, and the third is attempted here. There was, initially, the task of tracing the important neo-classical doctrines up from their source. Here, naturally enough, the intervening commentary of the French and Italians deserved and gained more attention than the text. Thus it contented Bray in his book on the rise of French neo-classical criticism to point to the origin of its critical ideas without comment upon the source itself.[3] The task Bray performed for French criticism was effected for English criticism by Saintsbury, Spingarn,

---

[1] *The Sacred Wood* (London, 1960), pp. 10-11.

[2] M.T. Herrick, *Aristotle's "Poetics" in England* (New Haven, 1930), p. 30.

[3] *La Formation de la doctrine classique en France* (Paris, 1961), passim.

and Atkins. Secondly, there was the job of examining the general affinity between the critical ideas of the English writers who dealt with Aristotle and the source from which, directly or indirectly, they drew them. This was done by Herrick. He extracted a body of doctrine (twelve points in all) from the *Poetics*, "in the light of the best modern interpretations" (p. 4), and applied his twelve-point scheme to the relevant English critics from the sixteenth century on. Here the text gained in importance, of course, but the precise extent of the distortion of the text and the detailed use made of it were not explored. It is, then, the aim of this study to give such a picture, to show six English neo-classical critics dealing with Aristotle face-to-face.

The procedure I have adopted here is the contrary of that used by Herrick, since his method would involve an unwarrantable amount of cross-reference and would obstruct the task of gaining an impression of each critic's individual handling of the text. Moreover, many of the passages selected for examination (particularly in Rymer) have such a narrow application that they would have to be neglected by a more general plan. The reason for this limitation may be traced to the method that the neo-classicists used to expound Aristotle. Bernard Weinburg's article, "From Aristotle to Pseudo-Aristotle",[4] explains what it was. Weinburg showed that the Italians began their exposition of Aristotle by using a system of line-by-line exegesis that had already been in operation on the *Ars Poetica* of Horace. They saw both works as belonging to a single critical tradition that had an essentially rhetorical bias: but in expounding both they gained no impression of the works as a whole, and both were thus completely fragmented. We may add to Weinburg's findings that the nature of many of the remarks in the *Poetics* is such as not to discourage this method of interpretation. The idea that poetry is more philosophical than history; that a work must have a beginning, a middle,

---

[4] Reprinted from *Comparative Literature*, V (1953); pp. 97-104 in *Aristotle's "Poetics" and English Literature*, ed. Elder Olson (University of Chicago Press, 1965), pp. 192-200.

and an end; that normally disgusting objects please in imitation--all these propositions belong to carefully sequential arguments, but they have an appeal in themselves that promotes any tendency to ignore their context. Thus the English critics who relied heavily on French intermediaries inherited a habit of study two centuries old.

So much for the method. What of the state of the text? It seemed desirable to investigate whether the text had undergone any significant changes since its rediscovery in the late fifteenth century, and to determine this I examined three versions widely separated in time and circumstance.

The earliest version was a sixteenth-century Latin translation, so literal as to be practically as useful as a Greek edition. This was made by Pietro Vettori and published as part of Averroes' Latin commentaries on Aristotle, as also in Vettori's own edition of the *Poetics* in 1560. This remained the best edition of the Greek for over two hundred years.[5] Both were used by the author of my second version, Dacier. He published a translation and commentary in French in 1692, which was anonymously translated into English in 1705. This was the first version in English and widely used on its appearance. The lateness of its date is a surprise to many.

It soon became clear that textual differences account for very little in assessing the enormous differences in its exposition. Though one main manuscript tradition (now represented solely by the MS. Riccardianus 46) was lost before Italian commentary got under way, at least two manuscripts that had been corrected from the Riccardianus did survive.

Furthermore, though Arabic, Syriac, and mediaeval Latin versions of the text have made some contribution to our knowledge since the beginning of the nineteenth century, the difference that these versions have made to our understanding involves the minutiae of readings--at a level of scrutiny the literary critics were not concerned to attempt.

---

[5] See my article, "British Editions of Aristotle's *Poetics* to 1794", *The Library*, 5th ser., XXX (September 1975), 238- 41.

Introduction

One recognises, too, that much sound editing was done by the Italians. Vettori himself is frequently cited in the *apparatus criticus* of the modern version I used (the Oxford Classical Text, edited by Kassel).

It is, then, the expectations, assumptions, and climate of the audience that accounts for the variety of response to Aristotle's "short and broken" treatise. The compactness of the text, amounting sometimes almost to incoherence, has compelled expansion, and that expansion has always taken colour from its context. In the neo-classical period in England these colours were at their brightest.

CHAPTER ONE: THOMAS RYMER

The style and temper of Thomas Rymer's critical writing present a problem in organisation that defies solution in the normal way. His handling of Aristotle has no consistent pattern, shows no signs of development or coherence, and indeed resists one's attempts to impose a pattern on it. In face of his position in formalist criticism in England this is slightly unexpected. He was prominent among those who laid stress on regularising critical principles and who relied on French critics in establishing what was proper to the canon of critical doctrine. The influence of the *Poetics* on the formulation of this canon was extremely powerful, and so one might well expect to find that Rymer gave it an integral and coherent role in his own critical writing. However, it is the direct influence of Aristotle's text that we are setting out to appraise, and that was not strongly felt in French criticism itself. From the French critics, and particularly from Rapin, with whom he had much to do, Rymer could gain little impression of the *Poetics* as a work with an identity of its own, deserving separate attention. We must look in Rymer, then, not for coherent patterns of ideas in which Aristotle plays a significant part, but at the seriousness underlying what is often a facetious style; at his depth of learning; and at the hard-headedness of much of what he writes. To each of these aspects of his criticism Aristotle has some relation.
    I have divided my examination into two main sections. The first examines his knowledge of the text and his opinion of Aristotle, and deals with the question of probability as it affects the foundations of his criticism. These are all matters of general nature, and the second section will deal more specifically with the use Rymer made of particular passages and remarks from the *Poetics*. I conclude with some general observations on the character of his work as Aristotle relates to it.
At the time Rymer began to write it was open to him to gain support and inspiration for his critical ideas on Aristotle from a number of sources: the text of the *Poetics* itself, or Italian commentary, French formalist criticism, or those in England who had already been affected by the continental writers. In

fact he turned to the French, as G.B. Dutton first indicated in detail in 1914.[1]

But from them he could have gained little direct information on the actual contents of the work, at least before 1692 when Dacier's translation and commentary appeared. The task of editing the Greek text had been thoroughly effected by the Italians, who produced the first printed edition of it in 1508. (There was no French edition of the Greek text before that of Batteux in 1771.) Furthermore Rapin, Rymer's chief mentor in the early part of his career, quoted from the Greek of the *Poetics* on only the rarest occasions. Indeed Joseph Warton remarked that Rapin had to rely upon a friend (Tanneguy le Fèvre, father of Mme Anne Dacier) to supply him with the Greek quotations he needed.[2] Rymer's own knowledge of the language is clearly more substantial than Rapin's can have been, even if it is also grammatically somewhat shaky. He quotes at some length from Apollonius Rhodius (pp. 10-11), translates Aristophanes with some zest (p. 95 ff.), and gives a *résumé* of the *Hippolytus* of Euripides that suugests an immediate acquaintance with the original (p. 50 ff.).[3]

Unfortunately he is less generous with quotations from the *Poetics*. To judge merely by the extent of his citation of the Greek, it would be conceivable that he never actually consulted the text in its original form. Nor can Averroes, or Scaliger, whom he also mentions on occasion,

---

[1] G.B. Dutton, "The French Aristotelian Formalists and Thomas Rymer", *PMLA*, XXIX (1914), 152-88.

[2] See *The Adventurer,* 49 [April, 1753], in *British Essayists*, ed. A. Chalmers (1923), XX, 44.

[3] All references are to C.A. Zimansky, *The Critical Works of Thomas Rymer* (New Haven, 1956), except where the short title *Reflections* appears, to denote Rymer's translation of Rapin's *Reflections on Aristotle's Treatise of Poesie* (the anonymous 1674 edition). Rymer's Greek quotations of the *Poetics* (seven words in all) may be found in Zimansky on pp. 23, 86, and 163.

have afforded him with much information on the Greek text. The question of his source must remain open.

Moving to Rymer's attitude to Aristotle, we may become more positive. For some years before Dutton's article (1914), opinion differed on whether Rymer was a rationalist critic, whose reliance was primarily on common sense, or a formalist, owing allegiance to the Rules. Spingarn and Saintsbury argued from different sides here, but Zimansky resolved the problem, pointing out that it is a slight one, since "common sense leads to rules and rules to a system" in Rymer's time.[4] This point is confirmed by Rymer's obvious approval of a remark in Rapin's Advertisement to his *Réflexions* (1674). Rapin (Rymer himself translated him) has it as follows:

> In effect this *Treatise* of *Poesie*, to speak properly, is nothing else, but *nature* put in method, and *good sense* reduc'd to principles.[5]

Rymer's own comment on this appears in his Preface of the Translator:

> The Truth is, what *Aristotle* writes on [poetry], are not the dictates of

---

[4] *Critical Essays of the Seventeenth Century*, ed J.E. Spingarn (Oxford, 1908-1909), I, lxv, lxxi; G. Saintsbury (in a flurry of metaphor), *A History of Criticism and Literary Taste in Europe* (London, 1900-1904), II, 392; Zimansky p. xxiii.

[5] *Reflections*, p. [b3r.]. Another work by Rapin, *De Carmine Pastorale*, was translated in 1684 by Thomas Creech and was reissued by the Augustan Reprint Society (no. VIII, 1947). In his introduction to this reissue J.E. Congleton misapplied Rapin's remark by making it refer to Rapin's own *Réflexions*. On the basis of this misapplication Congleton then made Rapin a member of the "School of Sense".

> his own magisterial will ... Nor would the *modern Poets* blindly resign to this practice of the *Ancients*, were not the Reasons convincing and clear as any demonstration in *Mathematicks*. 'Tis only needful that we understand them, for our consent to the truth of them. (pp. 2-3)

Rymer was the first in a line of critics, notably Dryden, Dennis, and Pope, to approve of Rapin's opinion. And one further piece of evidence is the more useful because it is indicative of a habit of thought about Aristotle the Schoolman, and not an explicit comment on Aristotle the Critic. Rymer can say, apparently with no danger of being misconstrued, that it is not necessary to be "some *Aristotle*, and *Doctor* of *Subtilties*" to judge what makes a good plot (p. 18). Good sense is enough for this, but good sense and Aristotle the critic belong together. The fact, then, that Aristotle's logic had been entirely superseded did not affect his authority as a critic.

So much for Rymer's good opinion. What about the relative critical standpoints of the two critics? To put these in perspective I wish first to compare Aristotle with Rymer on the distinction between poetry and history. Rymer gives, in all, three different versions of the pronouncement that poetry is more philosophical and serious than history, and one gloss on it. The gloss is perhaps the most interesting in relation to the development of critical ideas and the freedom with which they were manipulated. In his Preface to Rapin, Rymer declares that Aristotle thinks

> *Tragedy more conduces to the instruction of Mankind than even Philosophy it self.* (p. 2)

This is where Rapin had said, in his *Réflexions* (II, iv), that "*Poetry* proposes [virtue] free from all imperfections, and as it ought to be in *general*, and in the abstract. This made *Aristotle* confess that *Poesie is a better School of virtue, than Philosophy it self*". "Poesie" (epic/tragedy--which, or both?) shows virtue as it ought to be, presents morally uplifting exempla. This is a fact--not, we notice, a point that requires argument or the support of authority--and recognising it as such Aristotle was moved to say it gives Poesie an edge over philosophy. It is only from the context that it is clear that, in talking of "*Poesie*", Rapin had epic specifically in mind. Dacier,[6] however, in taking up Rapin's remark, made its application to epic explicit. Both critics allude to Horace as taking "less account of the *Lessons* of *Crantor* and *Chrysippus* (both philosophers), for the manners, than those of *Homer*"; but only Dacier allows it to be seen that the Horatian idea should be distinguished from the Aristotelian judgment. He remarks that "*Horace* has said more than *Aristotle*; for he asserts that an *Epick* Poem (which without contradiction is inferiour to Tragedy in that respect) is more Philosophical than Philosophy it self" (*Remarks*, IX, 5). Where Dacier redirects the emphasis by using an *a fortiori* reference to Horace and epic, Rymer goes in the other direction. He talks, as we have seen, about tragedy, not about "*Poesie*" or epic, and he ignores the distinction between Horace and Aristotle. But, if questioned, Rymer would surely have asserted that he had Aristotle's immediate authority for saying tragedy instructs better than philosophy does. Indeed, he would probably have made the remark about all three genres indifferently.

We now turn to Rymer's longest comment on a closer version of the pronouncement. We gain a good impression of his critical position as compared with Aristotle's. He writes as follows:

> *Aristotle* tells us, *That Poetry is something more excellent, and more philosophical, than History*, and does not inform us what has been done; but teaches us what may, and what ought to

---

[6] André Dacier's translation and commentary on the *Poetics* (1692) were published in an anonymous English version in 1705. I distinguished between the translation, where I cite chapter and section, and the commentary, to which the cue-title *Remarks* is given.

> be done. *Poetry* has no life, nor can have any operation without *probability*: it may indeed amuse the People, but moves not the *Wise*.   (p. 8)

The immediate application of these remarks is to Cowley's *Davideis*. Rymer criticises him for having taken a biblical subject, thereby involving himself in his fable with too much that is improbable and unaccountable. The Divine Dispensation, Rymer asserts, is inimical to the probability that should control poetry. The three salient features of Rymer's argument are (1) that poetry is superior to history; (2) that it teaches what should be done; (3) that its whole basis lies in probability. Because it is controlled by probability, it can teach; because it teaches, it is more excellent. The context of Aristotle's own argument is supplied by chapters VII and VIII of the *Poetics*. There he claims that poetry is shaped according to certain universal principles that determine beauty. Size (7.50b.34-7), unity (b25-31), and selectivity (8.51a16) are the most important of these. More particularly he argues that unity presupposes between its constituent parts a mutual and logical interdependence (7.51a11-15; 30-4). Only then does Aristotle remark:

> It is clear (from what has been said) that the job of the poet is not to speak of what has happened, but to speak of what might happen, and of the possible, according to probability or necessity. For the poet and the historian do not differ in that they speak in verse or without it ..., but in this, that the one speaks of what has happened, and the other of what might happen. Hence poetry is more philosophical and more worthy of attention than history; for poetry speaks about the universal, and history about the particular. (9.51a36-b7)[7]

---

[7] Unreferenced translations of Aristotle are my own.

From Aristotle's previous argument it is clear that the fusion of the aesthetic properties of a work of art with the subject-matter of a plot is effected for the poet by the selectivity open to him. Since he produces something beautifully shaped and ordered, he is not tied to particular details, nor to merely recording events. Thus the superiority of his kind of writing is guaranteed, as it were, by criteria and aesthetic principles not of his own choosing. The three basic propositions of Aristotle's argument may thus be stated as follows: (1) poetry (for the reasons given) speaks of what may happen; (2) it speaks according to probability and necessity; (3) it is more philosophical than history. If we now compare Rymer and Aristotle together, it is obvious that they both derive the superiority of poetry over history from its function, but that where Aristotle says that poetry *speaks* of what might happen, Rymer asserts that poetry *teaches* what ought to be done. Rymer's argument has no antecedents of the kind attaching to Aristotle's: the link between function and judgment is still made by probability, but Aristotle's aesthetic considerations, not explicit in his argument, are replaced by functional requirements.

The full extent of the difference this created between the two critics may be judged by the fact that the practical application of probability in Rymer's criticism is no less important than its theoretical status. Rymer's detailed criticisms of English drama have probability as the keystone of their argument. We find him saying, successively, that in contrast to *Rollo* even Aesop's fables have "a little *reasonable Soul* within" (p. 24), that the improbabilities of *A King and No King* set it below history (p. 41), that nothing in nature was ever as improbable as *The Maid's Tragedy* (p. 61), and that "never was any Play fraught, like this of *Othello*, with [so many] improbabilities" (p. 134). We need only to recognise that at the basis of this insistence on probability lies both the demand that drama instruct and the contention that it can do so only when consistently credible and intelligible--and Rymer's divergence from the aesthetic temper of the *Poetics* becomes plain. To focus on the divergence for a moment, we may say that Aristotle's is an observation rather than a judgment, when he says that poetry "speaks"; the whole neo-classical canon, on the other hand, was sustained by the contention that poetry "teaches".

Since, as has already been remarked, it is impossible to tie Rymer down to a coherent series of statements or attitudes regarding the details of the *Poetics*, and since he jumps so erratically from point to point, the best way to approach him is to range the topics to which the *Poetics* is relevant under general headings. From *The Tragedies of the Last Age* (1678) I take for discussion the relation between writing and acting, the question of when tragedy was perfected in Greece, the background to Rymer's views of poetic justice, and one further aspect of probability. From *A Short View* (1693) I look at the way in which Rymer sees drama make its impact on the senses, and at the place he gives to religion in tragedy.

First the relation between author and actor. Critics, Rymer thinks, need not only right judgment but also the ability to distinguish what pleases in itself from what may please because of exterior effect. He remarks that the popularity of *A King and No King* stemmed largely from the acting of Hart, the leader of The King's Company, and not from the writing. An aside here attributes a similar complaint to Aristotle. The same was true, says Rymer, in Aristotle's day, when there were "some who (wanting the talent to *write* what might *please*) made it their care that the *Actors* should help out, where the *Muses* failed".

Rymer's allusive and impressionistic way of writing makes it difficult to pin down a source. There are at least three passages that may be considered to offer him grounds for his assertion, but even the most plausible of them does not suggest any concern with its context.

Zimansky offered *Poetics* 14.53b7-8, without comment. There Aristotle says that "to produce [pity and fear] by means of spectacle is less artistic [than making it arise from the writing], and requires the use of a stage director". Here is an obvious affinity with what Rymer says, but none the less, if the passage is to stand as his source, "spectacle", must first be taken to relate specifically to the stage presence of the actors, and not to the whole visual impact of the play. It is not to be denied that Rymer could have used the technical term as loosely as this, and to this extent one could have no quarrel with Zimansky's citation.

But, on the other hand, if the relation between Rymer and Aristotle is to be as loose as this, then two further passages lay claim to consideration.

In one Aristotle says that good poets write episodic plots (the worst kind in his opinion) "because of the actors" (9.51b37). By this he means, either that the poet stretches his material to make it long enough to go on the stage,[8] or that he puts episodes in his play as a favour to an actor, on whom attention will naturally be turned during its course. At the first glance this may look somewhat unconvincing as an analogue for Rymer's saying the poet made sure that the actors assist him when his writing was poor. The relation seems to be the wrong way round, for Rymer maintains the poet cannot help his bad writing, whereas the passage we are examining says that the poet's lapse is deliberate. But this discrepancy between the critics turns out to be less damaging than at first appears. Given that Rymer is not reading the *Poetics* at all closely in any case, there is no reason why he could not have hit upon this passage, if (as seems plausible enough) he thought it implied that when a (good) poet writes poorly, as by definition he does if his is an episodic plot, then the actor is there to make a good impression.

One other possibility deserves attention. It is to be found in Averroes' loose paraphrase of the *Poetics*, with which Rymer was acquainted. As his version of the passage Averroes has the following:

> The really good poet must not make his imitation by means of exterior effect; this is to take on the function of an actor in gestures of face and body. False and pseudo-poets do this, who want to appear poets when they are not. Genuine poets do not do it unless they are endeavouring to battle against the practice of false poets.[9]

---

[8] See Ingram Bywater, *Aristotle on the Art of Poetry* (Oxford, 1909), p. 109.

[9] "Averrois paraphrasis in librum Poeticae Aristotelis, Iacob Mantino...interprete" in *Aristotelis Opera cum Averrois*

Since it is no harder to derive Rymer's idea from this part of Averroes' than from anything else we have so far examined, and since Rymer did know Averroes, we should perhaps allow this last passage as much countenance as the other two. But the real lesson of all this source-hunting is that it does not do to cite specifics from the *Poetics* at all hastily when Rymer offers Aristotle as a source, since there are likely to be many complications attached to what may seem a perfectly straight-forward allusion. Then, too, it is likely that the validity of any critical idea that Rymer advances will have to be determined intrinsically. Like all neo-classical critics, he thinks, of course, that Aristotle and reason go hand in hand, and to this extent what he cites purportedly from the *Poetics* will have its appeal as plain good sense. This is rather fortunate, not only for Rymer, but for his age too. The tenor and context of Aristotle's remarks very often tells against the critic who cites him, and the actual wording of the text is not infrequently plain contrary to what it is represented to be.

Our second point of detail concerns the history of tragedy that Rymer prefixes to his critique of *Rollo*. Although parts of chapter IV of the *Poetics* were almost certain to appear in the potted histories of tragedy, in the present instance, the contribution is slight. Rymer mentions only that Aeschylus and Sophocles increased the number of actors in tragedy, and that Sophocles, who introduced painted scenery, "gave (in Aristotle's opinion) the utmost

---

commentariis, secundum volumen: *De Rhetorica et Poetica Libri* (Venice apud Junctas, 1562; reprinted Frankfurt am Main: Minerva Verlag, 1962), pp. 221v.-222r. My translation. Rymer's references to Averroes read as follows: "*Averroes* rather chooses to blame the practice of his Countreymen as vicious, than to allow any imputation on the doctrine of [Aristotle] as imperfect" (p.3); "*Averroes*, after his Comment on the *Poetica*, allows that *Aristotles* Rules do not much concern the Arabian Poets" (p. 109).

perfection to Tragedy" (p. 22).[10] Rymer is justified in his claim, but not for the reasons he alleges for making it. He implies that it was because Sophocles introduced the third actor and painted scenery that Aristotle said he perfected tragedy. But before the notion that tragedy was perfected can be allowed its place in chapter IV, a much closer examination of the relevant details is necessary. The case has to rest on what Aristotle is taken to mean by saying that tragedy "stopped developing when it attained its own nature" (4.49a15). Aristotle eventually answered an important question that he had explicitly postponed when saying that tragedy stopped developing. He left it to be decided later whether or not tragedy was "all that it need be in its formative elements",[11] but stated that question would have two parts. It would need consideration, he said, πρὸς τὰ θέατρα, "in relation to the theatre", and αὐτό καθ' αὐτο, "in itself". Montmollin's analysis of the extremely complex and contorted twenty-fifth chapter of the *Poetics* showed that both parts of the question were answered.[12]

The chapter deals with the difficulties and faults common in poetry, dividing them into those that are inherent and those that are accidental. In other words, Aristotle there makes the same kind of distinction as he had suggested would be necessary in deciding about the perfection of tragedy. He distinguishes between a fault that may be called "inherent" (καθ' αὐτην), which occurs, to take an example, when the poet has tried to imitate something that lies beyond the range of his art, and one that is adventitious, which arises when the poet is not informed about a technicality that belongs to some province other than his own. Moreover, it is worse, aesthetically speaking, for him to make a bad imitation than to make the odd technical

---

[10] The remark on Sophocles' perfection of tragedy is all that survives in *A Short View* (p. 94).

[11] So Bywater, p. 13.

[12] *La Poétique d'Aristote: Texte primitif et additions ulteriéures* (Neuchatel, 1951), pp. 99ff.

blunder (see 25.60b15-32). Now we may assume, I think, that Aristotle would have remarked here on the weakness inherent in tragedy, if he had indeed thought the art had not been perfected. In fact he criticises only the manner in which the art is sometimes handled by poor practitioners, and makes no comment about weakness to which all might be subject. He does not argue that, though tragedy had stopped developing, it had not developed far enough.

For the answer πρὸς τὰ θέατρα we have to turn to 26.61b27 ff., where it is determined that the faults in tragedy that supposedly make it inferior to epic are in fact to be referred to poor acting: the genre itself is not to be condemned. Again the evidence suggests that tragedy had been perfected. Both the questions postponed have been given some kind of answer--even if we find the first answered only by our own deductions. Rymer, therefore, was right in his contention; but the fact that his opinion happens to coincide with Aristotle's is not in itself enough to allow us to assume that he came anywhere near seeing the ramifications of what Aristotle wrote. This consideration gains in importance when we realise that it is by no means immaterial to Rymer whether or not Sophocles perfected tragedy. It is of importance to him that Sophocles wrote good tragedies and was called "*Wise* Sophocles", since he supposes, in looking at the plays of his own time, that he must conclude that "mens brains lye not in the same place as formerly; or else Poetry is not now the same thing it was in these days of yore" (p. 18). Aristotle thus confirms an opinion for Rymer and helps to establish him in a position from which to attack.

Our third point brings us again to probability, this time to the question of historical plausibility in drama. It was an old problem, but decided in Italy rather differently than in England. Robortello and Castelvetro both had a low opinion of the mentality of the mob audience in their day and maintained that it had to be able to believe what it saw was certain fact. The former remarked that, if an emotional response was to be stirred in the audience, they had to know "that the matter fell out that way: hence, if the tragic fable contains an action that was not performed and is not true, ... it may perhaps move the minds of the hearers, but certainly less effectively [than if it were true]".[13] Rymer follows the same kind of reasoning and is even further from the *Poetics*, in connection with *Rollo:*

> no reason, I presume, can be given, why, having found an History, this Author should change the names; ...Aristotle tells it as extraordinary, of a *Tragedy* made by *Polemon*; where in both the *names* and *matter* were of his own *invention*; and yet it had the fortune to *please*. He also reminds us that a man is better pleased with the *picture* of an *acquaintance*, than of a person of whom we had never*heard*. And we generally observe, when one tells of an *adventure*, or but a jest, he will choose to father it on some one that is *known*, thereby to get attention, and gain more credit to what he relates. (pp. 23-4)

The first point Rymer makes here has no foundation in the text of the *Poetics*. Aristotle remarked of the *Antheus* of Agathon (I have been unable to trace the wrong ascription of the play to Polemon, whose name does not appear in the *Poetics*) that it was *natural* that it should have pleased its audience, since "even the known is known to but a few, and yet pleases all" (9.51b25-6). As for the "picture of an acquaintance" that a man is supposed to be better pleased with, Aristotle's argument tends in a very different direction. He does not say that a man will be better pleased if he knows the subject of the picture, but rather that he will be pleased by something other than the subject, if he does not know him. The workmanship and the colouring will catch his eye instead. It seems, then, that Rymer did have some familiarity with Aristotle's argument in chapter IV: it extended, however, only to his being able to recall that Aristotle makes his hypothetical observer exclaim in recognition of the

---

[13] My translation of the Latin, in *Francisci Robortelli ... in librum Aristotelis de Arte Poetice Explicationes* (Florence, 1548), p. 93.

subject--"why, that is so-and-so!" (4.48b17). It seems likely that Rymer remembered this phrase and thought it natural to conclude that the man unfamiliar with the subject would be less pleased at the painting than he who cried out. He did not trouble to check the passage, or had no immediate means of doing so, and thus had no chance of seeing that Artistotle distinguished between *kinds* of pleasure, and not *degrees*.

While the subject of poetic justice will concern us at some length in chapter IV, the way Rymer handles it is better accommodated here. When Socrates set up for morality, says Rymer, "his *Camerades* ... and *Confederates*", i.e. Sophocles and Euripides, found that the indifferent dispensations of Providence were made the subject of scandal by the atheists. The poets' fabricated world, therefore, had to set the matter to rights. Their world had to be one with a coherent and properly balanced moral order. Sophocles and Euripides

> knew indeed, that many things naturally unpleasant to the World in *themselves*, yet gave *delight* when well *imitated* [footnote: "Aristotle, *Poet*"]. These they consider'd as the picture of some deform'd old Woman, that might cause *laughter*, or some light, superficial, and *comical* pleasure; but never to be endur'd on serious occasions, where the attention of the mind, and where the heart was engaged. (p. 23)

Instead of reproducing the passages on unhappy and happy endings (the key sections for many later theorists), Rymer has here taken hold of two other remarks. The remark on things naturally unpleasant belongs to chapter IV and is closely related to that concerning "a picture of an acquaintance". Its contention is to show that men must delight in imitation, since even normally disgusting objects then give them satisfaction. They can learn something from a good imitation even of them. The "*deform'd* old Woman", on the other hand, can be seen as an echo of the πρόσωπον διεστραμμένον, the "distorted mask" of comedy, that causes laughter without giving pain. However, to emphasise

Rymer's privateering in the *Poetics* would be greatly out of place. Instead we should notice, and, I think, approve of, the racy impressionism of his sketch, recognising the facility with which he could combine disparate material into a whole. Aristotle is useful to Rymer when he affords him tit-bits of information. Indeed, the remarkable thing about his treatment of poetic justice as a whole is that it ignores Aristotle, even to the point of making inherited culpabiliity do duty for Aristotle's ἁμαρτία. Rymer grounds the horrors of Greek tragedy in the ancestral curse, and so is sharply to be distinguished from the majority of neo-classical critics, who made the moral defect of the hero the cause of his suffering. This aspect of neo-classical doctrine we shall leave to a later chapter.

One further item in *The Tragedies of the Last Age* is important in assessing Rymer's use of Aristotle. In his analysis of *The Maid's Tragedy*, Rymer finds it necessary to observe that Melantius and Amintor are in a dozen minds whether or not to fight one another. But, he asserts,

> when a Sword is once drawn in Tragedy, the Scabbard may be thrown away; there is no leaving what is once design'd, till it be thoroughly effected. *Iphigenia Taurica* went to sacrifice *Orestes*, and she desisted, why? she discover'd him to be her Brother. None here [in Euripides] are such Fools as by words to begin a quarrel; nor of so little resolution, to be talkt agen from it, without some new emergent cause that diverts them. No simple alteration of mind ought to produce or hinder any action in a Tragedy [footnote: "Arist."]. (p. 73)

The key phrase here is "new emergent cause", for it is clear that Rymer demands that a substantial change in the action of a play be produced only by something of greater significance than the mere whim of one of its characters. By asserting Aristotle's support for the principle, Rymer brings us for the first time to a part of the *Poetics* to which we shall have frequent recourse. This is chapter XIV, which contains

Aristotle's directives on how to handle the dire incident that lies at the core of the tragic action.

Tragedy, he says often, must deal with pitiable and fearful events; in chapter XIV he details what kind of event most successfully produces pity and fear. It is the murderous action, committed or intended, between blood relatives (πάθη ἐν ταῖς φιλίαις, 14.53b19-20). Aristotle starts by laying down the possible ways in which the act may be presented and then gives an order of preference to them. The criteria are action or the failure to act, and knowledge of the victim or ignorance of his identity. Of the possibilities, "to be about to act with knowledge, and then not to act" is regarded as the worst mode.[14] "To be about to act without knowledge and then not to act" is the best. The all-important difference between modes is constituted by ἀναγνώρισις, "recognition", a word to which it is possible and desirable to give the narrow sense of "recovery from hamartia", this latter being the original mistake in identification. Thus the "new emergent cause" in *Iphigenia Taurica* is Iphigenia's recognition that the stranger she is about to sacrifice is her brother.

Here Rymer seems closer to understanding the drift of Aristotle's argument than at any other point. Indeed, the principle he attributes to Aristotle is one that can only be elicited by a relatively close reading of the text. One has to see how the intervention of recognition affects the issue of the dire action in order to be able to state the matter as Rymer did. It cannot, of course, be ignored that here Rymer may well have been indebted to an intervening commentator; but even so, his contact with Aristotle is exceptionally close here.

Rymer was nothing if not up to date in his critical reading. His translation of Rapin came out in the same year as the French original, and the epistle dedicatory of *A Short View* written in 1692, mentions Dacier, whose *Poétique d'Aristote* appeared in that same year. Moreover, his is more than a passing acknowledgement, for both his references to Aristotle in the work are closely related to Dacier's

---

[14] This is made explicit at 14.53b37-8.

commentary. Early in chapter I of *A Short View* Rymer turns to the reintroduction of the chorus into French drama. He regards it as being primarily an adornment of the stage-- "a goodly Show". In connection with this aspect of its role he comments that

> *Aristotle* [footnote: "Poetica"] tells us of *Two Senses* that must be pleas'd, our *Sight*, and our *Ears*: And it is vain for a *Poet* (with *Bays* in the Rehearsal) to complain of *Injustice*, and the wrong Judgment in his *Audience*, unless these *Two senses* be gratified.   (p.85)

Once again a number of passages in the *Poetics* could be called in evidence to support Rymer's contention. Zimansky cited 14.53b3-6 ("The plot should be so constructed that any one who hears the events as they unfold will shudder and be moved to pity") and 15.54b15ff. ("Beware of offending against the sense-perceptions [αἰσθήσεις] that necessarily attend on poetry"), but he failed to indicate that it was Dacier's version of the latter passage that Rymer used. This reads as follows at the place in question:

> Il faut observer toutes ces choses, & outre cela satisfaire toutes celles que demandent les deux sentiments qui sont inséparables de la Poésie.
> (XVI, 11; p. 244)

Aristotle's αἰσθήσεις, "sense-perceptions", has here been glossed by a couplet from Horace that suits the occasion admirably. Horace remarks that "segnius irritant animos demissa per aurem / quam quae sunt oculis commissa fidelibus" (*Ars Poetica*, lines 180-1). However, Rymer did not stand by the principle for long: he passed almost immediately to a condemnation to "those cheating Sences, the Eyes and Ears, which greedily took in the impression from the *Show* ... tho there was no great matter of *Fable*, no *Manners*, no fine *Thoughts*, no *Language*" (p. 88). Such was his reaction to the fact that tradition had it that Cardinal Richelieu wept at a performance of *Thomas Morus*. Despite this fact, once again the Muses have failed, and Rymer will have none of it.

It was unfortunate that Rymer did not stay with Dacier's translation of the *Poetics*, because the continuation of the passage he took from Dacier recommends the poet to avoid inconsistency in the visual element of his play. Aristotle is far from recommending the poet to fill the eye with spectacle. Indeed he plays down the visual element, and actually remarks that to frighten the audience by using mechanical effects has nothing to do with tragedy (14.58b8-10).

The last passage to be examined here concerns Aristotle's defence of poets when they are accused of blasphemy. It involves the poet-philosopher of the sixth century B.C., Xenophanes, who is named by Aristotle, but there is an ambiguity in the phrasing that makes it possible to cite either of two fragments. Aristotle allows the poet to defend himself from the charge of impiety in terms that may be interpreted in either the following ways. The essential point is that Aristotle exculpates the poet, even though on one interpretation Xenophanes has to be made to criticise him, and on the other to offer an agnostic view.

At 25.60b35ff. the text can be translated thus: "it may not be the best thing [to speak scandalously of the gods], and it may not be true; it may even be wrong, as Xenophanes thinks it is. But at least men do say as much". The poet, we may assume, may thus be forgiven if he does. On this interpretation of the text, one would naturally refer to fragment 11, which remarks that "Homer and Hesiod have attributed all that carries shame or blame among men to the gods, and have recounted many lawless deeds concerning them--stealing, fornication, and deceiving one another".[15] On the other hand, the text may also be translated in the following way: "it may not be the best thing and it may not be true; but at least it is (as Xenophanes says) in agreement with the common opinion". To support this interpretation, one turns to fragment 34: (rendered here in the abominable

---

[15] For the Greek, see Diehls, *Die Fragmente der Vorsokratiker* (Berlin, 1922), I, 59-60. My translation.

verse of Dacier's translator): "Of Nature, and the Gods, none 'ere yet knew. / Or ever shall, that which is plainly true; / And if by Chance, he thinks h'as [sic] found it out. / He knows it not, it still remains a Doubt".[16]

When Dacier came to the passage, he made some alterations to the Greek, the most important of which were the introduction of Homer's name and the insertion of a comment of his own, determined by his citation of Xenophanes, fragment 34. Accordingly, the passage reads as follows in the 1705 translation:

> 'Tis thus that we salve what *Homer* has said of the gods; for it may very well be, that what he has said may be neither true, nor better after this manner; but he has followed that which was reported; and otherwise as Xenophon [sic] says, *Who is sure that he knows the Truth of his Way* [?][17]

Despite the fact that Dacier added Homer's name to the text, he still used fragment 34, and not fragment 11. This may well have been because he was not aware of the existence of the other fragment, but clearly he was also using this passage to make Aristotle defend Homer from the charge of impiety levelled at him by Plato. We come at length to Rymer. His version of the passage reads as follows:

> For every Cavil, against any thing devised by the Poets, in relation to the Gods, *Aristotle* [footnote: "Poetica"] proposed one general answer, That Critic need not be so fierce and positive to quarrel on that account, where all are in the dark, that

---

[16] For the Greek, see Diehls, I. 54.

[17] XXVI [given as XXVII], 9; p. 437. *"Xenophon"* is corrected to "Xenophanes" in the corresponding Remark (p. 434).

> neither Critick nor Poet know ought of the matter. We may grant that this answer is evasive; And may allow that *Aristotle* might not be so great a Divine as *Plato*; yet, doubtless our Modern Divines are a match for Plato: ... Who all hold with *Homer* and the old Poets that God may to good ends and purposes, make use of evil means, and instruments. (p. 107)

Rymer has been led here entirely by Dacier, failing to realise that Dacier's quotation from Xenophanes was an addition to Aristotle's Greek. Rymer did not have the advantage, open to later English critics, of the italics in the English version of Dacier. The English translator marked all those passages where Dacier had been too liberal with the text, and it is thus plain to see in the 1705 translation that the remark given to Xenophanes does not appear in the Greek text. As far as Rymer is concerned, then, Aristotle is a sceptic in matters of religion. The fact that on either interpretation of his text Aristotle defends the poet on grounds of common opinion is obscured from Rymer completely. This is perhaps as well: had Rymer been aware that Aristotle said "at least men say as much", he would have been faced with the situation where indeed there was "a scandal to the *Divine Providence*" (p. 22). It was to answer just this scandal, Rymer considered, that Sophocles and Euripides wrote their tragedies.

Talk of Rymer's "lively" criticism--and lively it certainly is--could be a cover for an attitude that recognised a certain entertainment in his style and allowed him little else besides. But there is too much soundness in his basic critical approach for one lightly to dismiss him. His reputation in his own time would have suffered less than it did had he kept his model tragedy, *Edgar*, to himself. Zimansky, more familiar than most with Rymer, says its badness is legendary (p. 218): to many the conspiracy of silence is perhaps a better guide to its worth. But whatever his talents as a playwright, when he turns critic, Rymer is no mere antiquarian dressing up dull and dry sentiment in a racy style. The substance of his criticism frequently reveals as much forcefulness in argument as zest in presentation. (Whether one would go as far as Eliot, who said that his strictures on *Othello* have never been properly answered, is another matter.)

Rymer's handling of Aristotle is typical of his critical method in general. It was not enough for him to be timidly, or non-committally, accurate and scholarly--indeed, it was not of his age to maintain the careful historical perspectives that would have been essential in treating Aristotle in a scholarly way. But the absence of precision and accuracy on historical matters might almost be said to have been a necessary condition of Aristotle's coming alive to Rymer. The more contextual awareness one has of what the *Poetics* says, the more closed off the text becomes. Sometimes it is difficult to relate the text even to what remains to us of Greek drama: on a really close reading it is impossible to make it speak to the dramatic conditions of the neo-classic age.

Where, then, do we find the affinities between Rymer and the text he alluded to so often? The most important of his critical principles is that the entire basis of good drama lies in coherence, intelligibility, and good sense. Probability, in other words, is the *sine qua non* of both criticism and creation, the technical means of giving drama the qualities Rymer found so often it lacked. In the context of probability Rymer finds himself at his closest to Aristotle. The *Poetics* offers him a wealth of illustration and sound principle. As we have seen, he maintains that if you begin an action in drama it must follow its course through, unless satisfactory motive arises for a change of intention. Then, too, the poet's medium is live, but its particular virtues--spectacle and verse--must further an end different in kind from themselves; there must be a sound plot with good sense at the bottom.

Aristotle's good sense recommended him to Rymer's age. It is not surprising, therefore, to find that Rymer gives attention to these aspects of the *Poetics*, leaving the technical terms and detailed discussion alone. He bequeathed the debate on poetic justice, for instance, to men of "more flegm and consideration" than himself. The typical French formalist, says Dutton (p. 168), "analyzed various Aristotelian dicta in the light of the Italian commentaries, and he wrought them into rules and built them up into definite systems. Rymer did not continue the work of codification; rather, he took the results of the codification [prescriptions on probability, plot, poetic justice, decorum] and applied them in his own criticism". In this chapter we have seen something of the role that the *Poetics* itself played in complementing the influence of French criticism on Rymer. If he had continued the work of codification, the *Poetics* might have played a more integral part than it did in his writing. We have found, instead, that the influence of the text was extremely local. Rymer comments at the end of *The Tragedies of the Last Age* that many "slips and mistakes too you meet withall, but *the fortune of* Greece *depends not on them*" (p. 76). We could add, as a rider to this, that there are many slips in his handling of Aristotle, but that his own critical validity is not seriously compromised by them.

CHAPTER TWO: JOHN DENNIS

Shortly after Rymer had published *A Short View*, John Dennis, himself well primed in Dacier's new treatise, also put pen to paper. The result was the liveliest of all his critical works, *The Impartial Critick: Or, Some Observations upon a Late Book, A Short View of Tragedy* (1693). The five brief dialogues it contained were handled with judicious attention to characterisation and setting, but they did not range very widely in subject-matter, and were by no means exclusively concerned with Rymer. Nearly all the scathing criticism of Rymer came in the introduction and first dialogue: the second dealt with Oedipus as portrayed by Sophocles and Dryden, the fourth and fifth with the chorus. Dennis believes that "it is much more easie to find Faults, than it is to discern Beauties. To do the first [which, he thinks, was Rymer's aim] requires but common Sence, but to do the last a Man must have Genius".[1] Dennis also disapproves of Rymer's critical style. It is much too facetious, he thinks, for the weighty business of criticism; besides, even where the reader can tell that Rymer is in earnest, he may still not be quite sure of the extent to which he owes the success of some points to a well-tuned piece of irony.

Dennis's own style tended, as his critical career progressed, to assume the opposite fault of a too ponderous seriousness (a feature that accords with Pope's telling name for him--Sir Tremendous Longinus). In *The Impartial Critick*, however, there is a fine blend of easy wit with eager criticism that does not leave him open to the charge he laid against Rymer. Moreover, the title of his work is apposite enough, since its defence of the way Dryden handled the character of Oedipus is by no means partisan. Lee and Dryden had remodelled Sophocles in a joint production in 1678, and to this extent Dennis is party to an Ancients versus Moderns debate. His comparison reaches a tempered preference for the original, though not without some qualifications to preserve Dryden's good name. The modern

---

[1] All references are to *The Critical Works of John Dennis*, ed. E.N. Hooker (2 vols, Baltimore, 1939). Here I, 13.

version, he believes, altered the character of Oedipus in a way that was "less suitable to the design of Tragedy, according to *Aristotle*'s Rules" (I, 19). Dennis's judgment here must be challenged in one particular; namely, where it involves the interpretation of Aristotle's *hamartia*. The basic situation is simple--the hero in any tragedy must maintain a balance between the extremes of vice and virtue. The doctrines of the *Poetics* and the neo-classicists are at one on this matter, but there is a further specification to be made of the hero's character, over which the two camps divide. In Neo-classicism it is necessary to establish the degree of guilt allowable in the hero and also to motivate his crime; and here, in Dennis's opinion, Dryden has not managed as well as Sophocles. Dryden's Oedipus is "just, generous, sincere, and brave" (ibid.), in short too good a man. Sophocles' Oedipus, on the other hand, is less virtuously endowed and, more importantly, rather led on by impudence than deceived by ignorance. Since the ignorance of Dryden's character is considered to be "invincible" and he is "Sovereignly Vertuous" in other respects, we can see that it will be difficult for Dennis to draw a moral from the modern version of the play.

The term "*hamartia*" is now taken to signify a mistake in judgment (or, to be more particular, a mistake in identification), and not a moral failing; and it is also noteworthy that Aristotle had precisely the *Oedipus Tyrannus* in mind when he invested the tragic hero with this quality. The narrower sense of the term is particularly well suited to the situation of this play. For us, then, it is inadequate to ground the great afflictions of Oedipus merely in the fact that he had an "imprudent" fit of temper at the cross-roads: it is more significant to point out that he did not know the identity of the old man whom he struck, and did not know who Jocasta was when he married her.

Imprudence, however, is the aspect that Dennis has to emphasise, in order to allow the moral element of the play to move into operation. On his terms, the play offers a caution to the audience to beware of being "drawn in by the like neglected Passions to deplorable Crimes and horrid Mischiefs" (I, 20). One wonders who Dennis is addressing: presumably the lesser sort, the groundlings, have not the sensibilities or the education to be touched. The Christian gentleman, whom Addison was soon to educate, seems no more promising a target. There is a credibility gap between the high moral tone and such darker passions as might lead even the Christian gentleman to "horrid Mischeifs". But it took Sam Johnson, with the right blend of piety and common sense, to see that religion was too high a subject for poetry. In Dennis's time, the high ground was to be seized by Jeremy Collier.

Dennis is again also representative of the main feeling of his times in disagreeing with Dacier about the suitability of the chorus for modern Drama. He opposed the Frenchman's enthusiasm, and where Rymer had first hailed it as a "goodly *Show*" and then grown cautious of it, Dennis dismissed it outright. In his fourth and fifth dialogues he rejects all the theoretical arguments in favour of reintroducing the chorus, because he thinks the arguments to support it are based on an inadequate grasp of essentials. The subject of tragedy, according to Aristotle, is the imitation of an action. But this action is carried on in the parts of the play *between choruses*, so that their role cannot be essential. They are excluded, by definition as it were, from an integral part in tragedy. Secondly, the end of tragedy is to excite pity and fear: but the choric intervals tend to alter the mood and pace of a play and thus lessen the impact that these emotions should make on the audience. Thirdly, the argument that it is the chorus that teaches the people morality should be looked at again. Morality must be conveyed to them by the fable, which must itself be invested with universal and allegorical properties.

These, in sum, are the main points of the fourth dialogue: the fifth quickly resumes the discussion. Dacier, Dennis remarks, had maintained that a chorus ties the dramatist to the unity of place and that the dramatic justification for their continuing presence on the stage lies in their being interested dependents of the protagonists. They are watching a "Publick and Visible Action" (*Remarks*, XIX, 27; Dennis, I, 36). Dennis categorically disclaims that this argument can be founded either on Aristotle or on the practice of the ancients. Neither is its corollary of any great value:

> An audience between the Acts should have a much better Security for the return of the Actors than Custom, and that is from the Nature of Tragedy, which is the imitation of an entire action ... which has a beginning, a middle, and an end.   (I, 39)

One notices all through these arguments that Dennis shares with Rymer the desire to put theory on a solid foundation of Reason. Aristotle is good sense reduced to a method. The evidence of *The Impartial Critick* suggests that Dennis was no less ready than Rymer to resort to Aristotle, as also to consult French sources (particularly Dacier) for knowledge of the text. We have still to determine, however, whether or not he had a greater disposition than Rymer to make independent inquiry and judgment. The evidence for this will be forthcoming in our examination of his later works.

In relation to Dennis longest critical piece, the *Remarks on "Prince Arthur"* (1696), I offer some general comments on the status Dennis gives to the fable of epic, and then wish to examine several passages in detail. Blackmore's poem itself will not be given any attention, since Dennis uses Aristotle only in the general lines of his argument. He does say that "Mr. *Blackmore* having own'd the Jurisdiction of *Aristotle*, is obliged to be tried by him" (I, 55), but the distance between what Blackmore wrote and what "reason suggested to [Aristotle], and what she repeats to us" is perceived to be very great. While, then, Dennis is applying his principles to a particular work, Blackmore comes so wretchedly off that he would be intrusive in the present discussion.

Dennis opens with Le Bossu's definition of epic and thinks that "it will not be amiss to explain it". To show how it is that epic constitutes "a Discourse invented with Art, to form the Manners by Instructions disguis'd under the Allegory of Action" (I, 55),[2] Dennis borrows from the two

---

[2] Dennis translates the *Traité du Poeme Epique*, I, 3. For the influence of this work on English criticism, see A.F.B. Clark, *Boileau and the French Classical Critics in England (1660-1830)* (Paris, 1926), pp. 243-61.

other French critics who are of outstanding importance for the influence of Aristotle in England. Rapin wrote that "the *design* of a Poem must consist of two Parts, of Truth, and of Fiction; Truth is the foundation, Fiction makes the accomplishment" (*Reflections*, I. xx; p. 26). Dennis says that epic fuses truth, which is the foundation of epic, and is of course moral, not historical, truth, with fiction, which disguises the truth under an allegory and gives it the form of a fable. Dacier leaning on Le Bossu (as he often did) contended that "there is no Fable, which was not invented, to form the Manners, by Instructions disguised, under the Allegory of an Action" (*Remarks*, VI, 8; p. 79); that the particulars of history do not match the experience of its readers, whereas the more general scope of epic allows it to reach all men (ibid., IX, 5); and that the universal and allegorical action of epic over-rides the particular actions of the poem. Dennis follows suit throughout. He remarks, for instance, that the "Historical" character of Aeneas is of very minor importance, if we think of the illustration he affords of the principle that "those good and great Men, of whom Heaven made choice for the Instruments of its great Designs, were highly favour'd and protected by Heaven; and that their Opposers were impious in vain" (I, 55-7).

It is evident, then, that Dennis is greatly reliant on French criticism in establishing the main lines of his argument, the preparation for his attack on Blackmore. But there is a further feature in the introductory sections of the *Remarks on "Prince Arthur"* that we should note. Dennis thought good sense alone was not sufficient for the making of a good critic. What then are we to conclude from the fact that, in these introductory sections, he contends three times in four pages that "Right Reason, as well as *Aristotle*", have led him to the position he adopts? There are three passages in his criticism which, if taken together, afford us a sound indication of the status of Reason in his writing. The application of the first is to the question of character portrayal, but we are at liberty to take it more generally.

> The Manners indeed are to be constant, not because *Aristotle* has said it; for to affirm that

would be absurd, but because Nature will have it so. For the Rules of *Aristotle* ... are but Directions for the Observation of Nature, as the best of the written Laws, are but the pure Dictates of Reason and Repetitions of the Laws of Nature. For either this must be granted, or *Aristotle* must be confess'd to have contradicted the Design which he had in prescribing those Rules: Which Design was to teach Men to please, more than they could do without these Rules ... And he who keeps up strictly to his Rules, is as certain to succeed, as he who lives up exactly to Reason is certain of being happy. But it is impossible for any man who has not a great Genius, strictly to observe the Rules ... I defie any one to show me a regular Epick Poem, or Tragedy which was not writ by a very extraordinary Man

(I, 96-7)

Good sense and Genius, therefore, are not antithetical terms, as Dennis's comment on Rymer might have suggested; they are complementary, and their being so elevates good sense above the prosaic. Furthermore, while there is, in criticism, an interdependence between good sense and genius, much akin to that between fancy and judgment, there is also a philosophical region where a similar interdependence obtains. In two later works Dennis suggests that "there is nothing in Nature that is great and beautiful, without Rule and Order" (*The Advancement and Reformation of Modern Poetry*, 1701; I, 202), and that "the Work of every reasonable Creature must derive its Beauty from Regularity ... The Works of God, tho infinitely various, are extremely regular" (*The Grounds of Criticism in Poetry*, 1704; I, 335).

Our examination of what Dennis owes to the *Poetics*, explicitly or by inheritance from the French, in his analysis of Blackmore's poem may be treated in four sections: firstly the (by now) surprising agreement between Aristotle and Le Bossu--and hence Dennis--on how the poet goes to work; then Dennis's discussion of the role of manners in poetry;

then his mention of how to handle dire incidents in tragedy; and finally the problem of how the business of imitation is to be approached.

When Clark documented the waning of Le Bossu's reputation in England (pp. 265 ff.), he showed that the idea that the poet began with a moral and built his poem around it, frequently came in for adverse criticism. But unappealing as the idea was to non-formalists, its supporters nevertheless could find the germ of the notion in the *Poetics*. Their proximity to Aristotle on this topic may not have been consciously recognised by the neo-classicists, but it strikes us--largely because Aristotle's own analysis does not ring true. Aristotle makes a division between the main outline of a story and the details that will attach to it in terms that suggest mechanical operation. He remarks, for instance, that "after [making his general synopsis], the poet may add the names and fill out the episodes" (17.55b12-13; cf. 9.51b9-10). Thus, in Aristotle's view, a poem will cohere only if the poet is not distracted by details of minor circumstance and by names.

One can accept that the Greek tragedians must have begun with an overall vision of the direction they wanted their plays to take, and thus did work at some stage with what we would regard as the theme in mind. But they can have had far less scope for free invention than Aristotle's directive implies. Once their choice of story had been made, they must have found themselves involved with traditional material to which few substantial alterations could be made. Even by the time they had reached what Aristotle calls the synopsis, they would have had to stop thinking in abstract terms. Furthermore, there are passages in the *Poetics* that say both that the poet need not regard himself as being restricted to completely traditional material (9.51b23-5), and that he must stand by it (14.53b22-3). In the former case, the poet is released from obligation, because "even the known names are known to but a few", names being secondary for Aristotle. But in the latter case, the poet is bound to the observation of a principle, because he cannot decide merely for himself who shall be killed. Finally, even though Aristotle himself gives a model synopsis of the general outline of *Iphigenia Taurica* and of the *Odyssey*, the terms in which the synopses are given make them applicable only to their respective titles.

The mechanical emphasis of this part of the *Poetics* is admirably suited to Le Bossu's doctrine. Aristotle makes the poet begin with a general statement of his aims; for Le Bossu and many in his age the aim must be the inculcation of a moral; accordingly, around the moral all the remaining details and circumstances of a play will form themselves. The characters, in Dennis's words, "remain at the bottom Universal and Allegorical" (I, 58). The neo-classical view of the nature and function of the plot determined the way in which Aristotle was interpreted on character. Our first task, then, will be to say something of his handling of this.

The translation seems to be Dennis's own, and there is no evidence that he took his Greek from either Le Bossu or Dacier, with whose his own translation shares some errors. The Greek appears as follows:

ἕξει δὲ ἦθος μὲν ἐὰν ὥσπερ ἐλέχθη
ποιῃ φανερὰν ὁ λόγος ἢ ἡ προαίρεσίν
τινα ... ἔστιν δὲ παράδειγμα πονηρίας μὲν
ἤθους μὴ ἀναγκαίου [οἷον ὁ Μενέλαος ὁ
ἐν τῳ 'Ορέστῃ]. (15.54a17-19, 28-9)

I have completed the sentence, since the latter part is essential for the understanding of what Aristotle says. But first a word about the readings. Of the significant Greek manuscripts only three read ἀναγκαίου (a29). All others read ἀναγκαίον to agree with παράδειγμα, and many editions read ἀναγκαίας to agree with πονηρίας.[3] In other words the sense of the passage is either "there is an unnecessary example of baseness of character...", or "there is an example of unnecessary baseness of character...". Dennis's version of the Greek would translate as follows:

---

[3] See the *apparatus criticus* in Montmollin, p. 255, for the readings, and E. Lobel, *The Greek Manuscripts of Aristotle's "Poetics"* (London, 1933), p. 46, for the position of the MSS in the tradition. It is not possible to determine the edition that Dennis was using.

"there is an example of baseness of character (the character itself being unnecessary)", which would make poor sense, if any. His actual translation does make sense, but at some cost to the wording of the Greek. It reads as follows:

> Then the Manners are good, when a Person shows by his discourse or by Actions, what choice or what resolution he will take ... The Manners when they are not necessary, are Poetically bad.   (I, 77)[4]

His version (a) ignores the μὲν/δὲ/δὲ antithesis of a28, 30, 31; (b) excludes the allusion to the *Orestes*, and so ignores the link παράδειγμα ... οἷον at a28-9; (c) has a genitive complex as subject of a sentence ("unnecessary manners are..."); (d) gives to πονηρία an aesthetic sense ("Poetically bad"), when the word is used only on medical or moral contexts in classical Greek. Dennis thus makes Aristotle plead for consistency, when in fact he is demanding goodness of character. It is somewhat ironic that notwithstanding the neo-classical emphasis on morality and improvement in poetry, Aristotle is misconstrued on one of the few occasions when he himself makes a moral demand. However, the emphasis on consistency is not in itself at variance with Aristotle's purposes. Nor, ultimately, is the demand for the intelligibility that character brings to action. It is rather the relative importance given to this factor which sharply distinguishes Aristotle from his commentators in the neo-classical period.

In his book, *On Aristotle and Greek Tragedy* (London, 1962), John Jones presented an impressively argued case for the revision of our whole notion of what Aristotle meant by "character" (ἦθος). He suggested, for example, that if Aristotle had had anything like our notion of "character", or had shared with us a psychological interest in it, then he was outrageously obtuse in his priorities. Aristotle says, after all, that it is because tragedy is an imitation of an action that there must be people to perform that action (2.48a1-2; see Jones, p. 14). Furthermore, Jones remarked,

---

[4] Cf. Dacier, XVI, 5; Le Bossu, IV, 4.

if Aristotle thought as we do about "character", it would also be most odd that he calls later Greek drama "characterless", when there is a marked increase in it both in naturalism and in concern with character portrayal (see Jones p. 32). For a variety of reasons, then, our notions of what character is must be relegated firmly to the back of our minds (and this includes our conception of the tragic hero), if we are to understand what ἦθος signified for Aristotle. In the foreground we should place Aristotle's contention that the actors "assume character for the sake of the action; they do not perform actions for the sake of imitating character" (6.50a20-2). It has been habitual to think that character occupies a second position in the parts of tragedy, between plot and thought: Jones maintains that character does not have even a subordinate position, since it has no autonomy whatever.

This consideration, however, is one that cannot be referred with any profit to neo-classical criticism. It is better, I believe, to take a hint from Crane, who pointed out that the neo-classicists placed the major parts of drama--plot, character, diction, and thought--in such tight compartments that critical discussion of them was mutually exclusive.[5] By virtue of this separation of one part from another in critical discussion, character was able to assume an autonomy that Aristotle had never conceived for it. Furthermore, where character was not considered merely in isolation, there was a strong tendency for it to become an embarrassment. But while it might have been a convenience to some English critics to concede plot its supremacy rather than to challenge Aristotle's order, none the less the English plays they were dealing with made plot of minor importance in comparison with character. The supremacy could be no more than merely theoretic. Of the critics with whom this study deals, only Harris mentions that character should exist for the sake of action (see *Philological Inquiries* (1781), in *Works* (1803), IV, 211 n.); almost as little attention was given to the

---

[5] R.S. Crane, "The Concept of Plot and the Plot of *Tom Jones*", in *Critics and Criticism* (Chicago, 1952), p. 617n.

proposition that tragedy can exist without character, but not without action (6.50a23-5).

The role that Dennis assigns to character is entirely conveyed by plot and action. He explains the link when he remarks that "an Action instructing by its causes, which causes are the Manners, unless I can be certain, what the principles of the Agents are, I can never deduce any certain Moral from the Action" (I, 42). Clearly, then, it appears to speak directly to his case when Aristotle says that "then the Manners are good, when a Person shews ... what resolution he will take".

Those of Dennis's readers who were familiar with the *Poetics*, and particularly those who knew it through Dacier, might have noticed the way in which certain other facets of plot and character were handled in the *Remarks on "Prince Arthur"*. Of the requirement that character be consistent, for instance, Dennis says that "when a Poet introduces any ... notorious [i.e. Historically or traditionally famous] Person, he is to paint him with the very same Qualities, which he is known to have had" (I, 72). Such a requirement would set the poet on some historical researches, of course; but, when these had been accomplished, he had then also to make the character's image larger and better than the life. Moreover,

> in order to the giving this best Likeness, a Poet is not so much to consult Nature in any particular Person, which is but a Copy, and an imperfect Copy of Universal Nature; he is to examine that Universal Nature, which is always perfect, and to consult the Original Idea's [*sic*] of things, which in a Sovereign manner are beautiful. This is the Precept of *Aristotle*, and his Interpreter *Horace*.
> *Respicere exemplar vitae, morumque jubebo Doctum imitatoram et veras hinc ducere voces.*[6]
> (I, 73)

---

[6] *Ars Poetica*, lines 317-18. Not infrequently *vivas* is read for *veras* in the second line.

Now the informed reader, as he read this, might have cast his mind back to Aristotle's advice that the poet "must imitate the good painters. For they, giving a man his characteristic appearance, paint him like he is and more handsome as well" (15.54b9-11). But he might have paused longer, when he considered how Dennis thought this had to be done. The recommendation to examine "Universal Nature, which is always perfect", and to "consult the Original Idea's of things", might have struck him as good advice coming from a Platonist, but less easily reconciled to the *Poetics*. He would remember that Aristotle had defined the universal as "the sort of thing it happens to a sort of person to say or do according to likelihood or necessity" (9.51b8-9), and perhaps conclude, from the total absence of metaphysics and philosophical speculation in the *Poetics*, that Aristotle was being distorted somewhat. However, we have already posited of our reader that he might have been familiar with Dacier as well as Dennis. He would thus possibly have found that Aristotle's advice to the poet to copy good painters was commented upon as follows: "[the poet] ought rather to work after Nature, who is the true Original than to amuse himself with any particulars, which is only an imperfect and confused Copy" (*Remarks*, XVI, 24; p. 274). He would then have had to decide how far Aristotle and Dacier differed in their advice.

Aristotle certainly suggests some idealising of the image and, at 25.60b32 ff., he does allow the poet to defend his picture of life from any of three positions--that it is ideal (b33), that it is in accordance with common report (b35), or that it is true to reality (b34). None the less, the concept of the perfection of Universal Nature has a closer affinity with the Platonic theory of Forms than the Aristotelian theory of Universals. What would the technical correlative to "working after Nature" be? Clearly, whatever images formed in the brain of the poet as a result of his having considered the "Original Idea's of things", the task of reducing them to actual passages of writing would involve him closely with the neo-classical conception of decorum. Now, Dacier's advice is itself made in connection with chapter XV of the *Poetics*, this being the section that lays down the famous four basic requirements for character--that it be good (χρηστόν), that it be suitable (ἁρμοττόν), that it be similar (ὅμοιον), and that it be consistent (ὁμαλόν). Thus, in "giving this best Likeliness", the poet will work within the body of doctrine elaborated upon in chapter XV. Its actual interpretation, however, was determined in accordance with Horace and the rhetorical tradition. The question, therefore, of the philosophical grounding of Dennis's advice to the poet is less immediately concerned with Aristotle than appears from his quotation. The idea itself must be referred directly to Dacier; the more significant technical considerations accompanying it, to the neo-classical concept of decorum.

It will be argued more than once that the philosophical background to the *Poetics* in neo-classical criticism comes not from Aristotle's own philosophy, but from a certain "pious sagacity" (to adopt Fielding's words in *Tom Jones*, VIII, i) in the age. We have had an instance already in this chapter of the kind of writing I have in mind, when Dennis drew his analogy between living by Reason and writing by the Rules; we will encounter more of it in Addison and Trapp. This species of writing, natural to the temper of the age and combined with the neo-classical inheritance from the rhetorical tradition based on Horace, provided Dennis with the grounding on which to rest Aristotle's treatise. Some such support was required, for the *Poetics* could not be read with any regard to the philosophical context within which it was written--that had to wait for S.H. Butcher.

In this early part of Dennis' critical career we have found him to be heavily reliant on Dacier's representation of Aristotle. In his next two extensive pieces of criticism, he makes less frequent use of Aristotle. But where he does employ him, the terms on which he is cited seem to have become Dennis's own. We will be looking in this section at his argument for the grounding of poetry in religion, and at his discussion of what kind of emotion is proper to tragedy.

The Advancement and Reformation of Modern Poetry (1701) extends Dennis's rationale of poetry along fresh lines. He announces the intention of mediating between its supporters rather than of defending it from detraction, as he had done in *The Usefulness of the Stage* (1689). Although his position favours many of the terms on which the Moderns argued, Dennis does concede a superiority to classical writers in one respect. This concession leads him to look for a new beginning rather than a reconcilement between parties. The ancients are not innately superior, he thinks; it is rather that their advantage lies in the fact that they took religion as the subject of their poetry. If the moderns would only found their poetry on this noble basis, they would surely equal, and might well surpass, the best that the ancients produced. In other words, they are to join Passion with Religion. Part of Dennis's argument for religion in poetry runs as follows:

> Tragedy, says *Aristotle* in his *Poetick*, is the Imitation of an Action which excites Compassion and Terror. Now those two Passions proceed from Surprize, when the Incidents spring one from another against our Expectations, For those Incidents, continues the Philosopher, are always more admirable, than those which arrive by Chance ... even of accidental Things, those are always the most Wonderful and most Surprizing, which at the same Time that they arrive by Chance, seem to fall out by Design, and by a certain particular secret Conduct; of which Nature was what they relate of the Statue of *Mitys* at *Argos*, which fell upon his Murderer, and kill'd him upon the Spot, in the midst of a great Assembly: For that by no means, says the Philosopher, seems to be the Work of Chance. From whence it follows, says he, of necessity, that those Fables where there is this Conduct, will always seem preferable to those that have it not. Thus *Aristotle* declares, That the Wonderful in Tragedy, as well as in Epick Poetry, is heightened by Religion, that those Tragical Incidents that appear to have most of Providence in them, are always most Moving and Terrible.
>
> (I, 30)

Dennis has given an accurate and complete paraphrase of *Poetics*, 9.52a1-11, and has drawn certain conclusions from it to support his case. It is noticeable that he is very careful to continue to indicate that he is quoting from Aristotle. All the evidence is thus before us when he comes to say "Thus *Aristotle* declares ...". However, had Dennis gone on to add that the scepticism of the heathen, evident in the phrases "*seem to fall out*", "*seems* to be the work of Chance", "Tragical Incidents that *appear* to have most of providence in them" may be excused, it would have been very helpful. He could have added that the Christian will firmly hold to the presence of God in Human affairs; but, without this rider, Aristotle's support is questionable.

It is quite clear that Aristotle gives no explicit assent to the moral implied in the story of Mitys, and therefore certain that he would not draw from the story anything like what Dennis saw in the *Aeneid*: that "those good and great Men, of whom Heaven made choice for the Instruments of its great Designs, were highly favour'd and protected by Heaven; and that their Opposers were impious in vain" (I, 56-7).) To help Dennis, the *Poetics* ought to reveal that Aristotle believed that the Mitys story would teach some such Providential lesson. However, if we turn to a companion passage to the one Dennis cites, we find that Aristotle's scepticism merely becomes more manifest.

The passage that Dennis has quoted deals with the marvellous in tragedy (τὸ θαυμαστὸν, 9.52a4-5): a much later section deals with the irrational in epic (τό ἄλογον, 24.60a13). It is in this later section that Aristotle says that Homer taught poets to "lie as they should", by using a device which Aristotle calls παραλογισμός, "false reasoning". By the use of this device, people are led, because they know for certain that B is the case, to believe (mistakenly) that A is true as well. In other words, we may say, because the statue that fell on the man was that of Mitys, the man having murdered Mitys, the gods *must* have pushed the statue over. Now, admittedly the example of Mitys belongs to chapter IX and not to chapter XXIV, but there is every reason for believing that the same principle holds. Furthermore, there is another difficulty in having the Mitys story appear where it does. Aristotle says that pity and fear arise best when the incidents embodying them are both surprising *and* logically connected (53a3-4): he continues by remarking that among events that *do* happen by chance, i.e., not from a logical relation determined by probability and necessity, those that are most surprising appear to have happened by design. The wording of this passage is such that the latter proposition has all the marks of being an *a fortiori* argument for the former. One is a recommendation, the other the argument to support it. Now the Mitys story, being an instance of an event that did arrive by chance, belongs to the *a fortiori* argument rather than to the recommendation: "even of those things that arrive by chance those seem most marvellous that appear to be by design-- as, for instance [the story of Mitys]". Finally, the passage concludes with a summary of the recommendations, and it is this summary which is the important thing. In it Aristotle says that "necessarily such stories will make the best plots". But though it is not immediately clear, Aristotle does not thereby recommend the Mitys story as a good plot. He must have known that Mitys had been killed in a feud, so that the poet who handled the Mitys story would be faced (in accordance with the recommendations of chapter XIV) with a dire incident that involved enemies. Aristotle's comment on such dire incidents is that they have "nothing pitiable in them either in the intention or in the action, except the deed itself" (14.53b17-18).

With the Mitys story thus properly evaluated, we may now note that Aristotle's actual recommendation in the passage Dennis cites is of events that contain "surprise", and actual, rather than seeming, logical relation. When examined carefully, then, it is found to contain nothing to support Dennis's missionary purposes, unless of course one adds (as Dennis does not) the qualification that scepticism of the heathen must be replaced by the assent of the Christian.

Dennis justified tragedy on so many different grounds in *The Usefulness of the Stage* that it is not surprising he gave no all-embracing principle to account for its operation. For *The Grounds of Criticism in Poetry*, however, he formed an ambitious plan that could have produced such a principle. As it was, he found himself hampered by a poor response in subscription, and the work did not progress far. He did, however, begin it by distinguishing between the passions involved in poetry, as being either "vulgar", or "enthusiastic", both laudatory terms. There is no more than a bare statement of his meaning apart from one illustration. The sun, he remarks, appears in ordinary experience as a round, flat, shining disk; but in meditation it becomes the most splendid and awesome of the objects of the visible creation. Poetry employs both responses, but since all men are capable of feeling the ordinary reaction, it should rule:

> perhaps this might be one Reason, for which *Aristotle* might prefer Tragedy to Epick Poetry, because the Vulgar Passions prevail more in it, and are more violently moved in it; and therefore Tragedy must necessarily both please and instruct, more generally than Epick Poetry.
> (I, 339)

Here there are no more than tentative parallels, and Dennis is himself tentative on the point. In fact the sole point of obvious agreement Dennis and his supposed source is that they both assert that tragedy is more immediate in operation than epic. "[Tragedy] has all that epic does ... and then vividness too, both in reading and in action" (26.62a14-18). Thereafter the two critics part company. "Vulgar" does carry a sting for Aristotle. He suggests that one might consider whether epic or tragedy is the superior genre and posits that,

> if the less vulgar (φορτική) is better, and if this is the kind addressed to the better audience, clearly an art imitating everything will be vulgar. (26.61b26-9)

Athens had its mob audiences, too, and Aristotle speaks elsewhere of the poets pandering to them (13.53a34-5). Here, however, the criticism of tragedy--that it is indiscriminate in the imitation it makes--is turned away from the genre onto bad actors. Excessive gesticulation and over-acting have given tragedy its bad name; the fault is not inherent in the genre. Aristotle, then, decides the question of superiority on certain criteria of form, and there is no real parallel between what Dennis means and what Aristotle means by "vulgar"; no real answer in the *Poetics* to Dennis's surmise, even in general terms.

One expedient would be to argue that epic is addressed to the "better" audience, "better" being actualised in "minority". This, at least, would imply that tragedy had the wider appeal, and their wider appeal induces Dennis to prefer the vulgar passions. But even having taken Dennis thus far, we would still have to cry halt before he reached the point he aims for. The Horatian doublet "please and instruct" cannot be applied with any profit to the *Poetics*, and it is precisely on this double criterion that Dennis grounds his preference, hoping for Aristotle's agreement with him.

We can observe Dennis on a very different moral tack, though engaged in a standard neoclassical procedure, in his occasional piece, *A Defence of Sir Fopling Flutter* (1722). He admits that the play is "an Imitation of corrupt and degenerate Nature"--but, says the redoubtable moralist, there is no adultery, murder or sodomy in it. Then comes a clear echo of Dacier's translation: Aristotle says that comedy imitates "Not the worst ... in every Sort of Vice, but the worst in the Ridicule". This is precisely the phraseology of the English translation of Dacier, to which Dennis adds that "a modern Critick" maintains that the comic poets "always took Care ... that those several Villanies [Adultery, Cheating, Theft, Murder] should be envelop'd in the Ridicule, which alone ... could make them the proper Subjects of Comedy". Dacier's argument (*Remarks*, V, 1) is in fact more contorted than Dennis's rendering of it reveals. Dacier has to deal with the fact that Horace (*Satires*, I.iv.3-5) claims that Greek comedy introduced just such dire "Villanies" as this, and that "Notwithstanding, Theft, Adultery and Murder are Vices which surpass Ridicule ... and so *Aristotle*'s Rule is not true". Inevitably such a challenge to Aristotle's authority cannot be allowed to stand--though Dacier's way of dealing with it is thin enough. He points to Aristophanes "ridiculing" Socrates when showing him "suspected of Impiety":"'twas his chief care so to hide those Vices under the Ridicule, that they might only appear thro' it". Despite his wish to solicit Dacier's aid, Dennis must have seen how thin the argument was. The consequence of leaving it alone, however, was to make it appear that murder and sodomy, *inter alia*, do indeed lie within the reach of ridicule--an implication which the stance he wishes to adopt does not require, in any case.

Before reaching our conclusions on the place of the *Poetics* in Dennis's criticism, we should look at a realignment of his early belief that the main virtue of Aristotle was his having made observations based on nature. In his *Causes of the Decay and Defects in Dramatick Poetry* (1725)[7] Dennis is as polemical a champion of the Rules as ever. His occasion of writing is partly to provide an answer to Leonard Welsted, who had dismissed the Rules very contemptuously, thinking them to be no more than a set of very obvious precepts. Not only this, he had the temerity to suggest that history was more generally useful than poetry.[8] What Dennis says in reply to Welsted may also be taken as a useful answer to a question that Hooker, Dennis's editor, poses in his introduction to Dennis's critical works. He asks "why should the regularity of Nature be reflected by the particular precepts of Aristotle rather than by a thousand other conceivable systems that would make for regular and orderly art?" (II, lxxxiv). Hooker answers his question, as we shall see shortly. But Dennis answers it too. He considers that poetry, if truly an art, must have a system. Furthermore,

> that System must be known. For there can noe more be an Art, that has a System of Rules which are not known, than there can be a countrey which hath a Body of Laws that are not promulgated. But there is for Poetry noe system of known Rules but those which are in Aristotle and His Interpreters, and therfor if

---

[7] Hooker argued for this date in *ELH*, I (1934), pp. 156-62: "An Unpublished Autograph Manuscript of John Dennis".

[8] See "A Dissertation concerning the English Language, the State of Poetry, Etc." (Preface to *Epistles, Odes, Etc.* (1724), in *Eighteenth-Century Critical Essays*, ed., Scott Elledge (2 vols, Ithaca, 1961), I, 326, 339.

> They are not the Rightful rules poetry is not an
> Art. (II, 283)

No one in Dennis's age realised a system that offered both a serious challenge to Aristotle and the possibility of reducing art to order and coherence. Hooker was thus right to answer his question thus:

> To Dennis the rules of Aristotle were empirical and scientific, they were laws describing how the human mind operated under certain circumstances, and they were based upon observation and understanding, and they had been confirmed by the experience of the ages.
> (II, 504)

Dennis was right in justifying Aristotle in the terms used in *The Decay and Defects*--so long as he included "His Interpreters" in his defence. Indeed, his reliance on them makes it impossible to determine the extent to which he read the *Poetics* without their aid. We have to balance the fact that the one passage he gives at any length in the original is accompanied by a gross distortion of its sense, against the consideration that he glosses a large section of another chapter without the aid of commentary.

Even so, his literal accuracy in representing the text compares favourably with Rymer's, and the use he made of his knowledge is markedly different. Rymer tended to pick up the odd phrase: Dennis advances central doctrines. Unlike any other in his age, Dennis maintains distinction between Aristotle and his commentators. He is also more scrupulous in his acknowledgements. The question posed earlier, as to whether Dennis showed a greater disposition than Rymer to study the *Poetics* directly, can be answered in the affirmative. His numerous references to Aristotle (there are over fifty of them) owe much to Dacier; but, the *Poetics* must always have been close at hand when he wrote. While, then, one would not for a moment dispute the importance of Longinus to his critical ideology, the *Poetics* was scarcely less influential upon this sometimes ponderous critic.

CHAPTER THREE: JOHN DRYDEN

> There are those who regard as the final test of an idea its coherent relation within a unified system. Dryden preferred to see it tested in a vigorous combat with its opposite, each side putting forth its utmost force. He wrote, accordingly, not treatises, but essays and dialogues.[1]

If, Dryden prefers vigorous combat to coherent relation, his critical method will almost certainly tend to reinforce the practice of his age when reading the *Poetics*: his exegesis will have no intrinsic tendency to counter the fragmentation to which the text was subject in his time. Dryden will be also unlikely to give to the *Poetics* a systematic analysis in any case, because the acceptable interpretation of Aristotle has already been made for critics who, like him, used the *Poetics* in contexts where practical literary concerns were uppermost. *Prima facie*, therefore, we might well expect to find that Aristotle is just as disembodied in Dryden's criticism as he was in Rymer's. At least, the cause for his not being so, must be rather in his critical temperament than in his critical method (to call it such). Indeed, it will be clear from what follows that his scepticism and his partiality for maintaining critical balance greatly affected both his use of the *Poetics* and his attitude to Aristotle. These two factors, scepticism and caution, result in a diffidence in the face of authority. Dryden has a considerable admiration for Aristotle, but one that is tempered by strong reservations, and he always feels it open to him to change his mind on matters of critical principle. For various reasons, we will find, Dryden keeps Aristotle at a distance.
      Perhaps the best indication of Dryden's independent attitude lies in his growing preference for heroic poetry over tragedy. In *An Essay of Dramatic Poesy* (written 1665-6) the superiority of tragedy is not in doubt. It is "by Aristotle, in

---

[1] L.I. Bredvold, *The Intellectual Milieu of John Dryden* (Ann Arbor, 1914), p. 13.

the dispute betwixt the epic poesy and the dramatic, for many reasons he there alleges, ranked above it".[2] Now, admittedly the *Essay* is a dialogue, and here especially one opinion must be balanced against another. But on this point, Dryden's preference seems to be clear. One finds, for instance that in *The Author's Apology for Heroic Poetry and Poetic Licence* (1677) Dryden echoes Rapin in calling epic the greatest work of man, and he also maintains that "in that rank has Aristotle placed it" (I, 198).[3]

The challenge to Aristotle's actual preferences is not very explicit, but none the less it is there. To this extent Aristotle is misrepresented. Even so, the question remains open, since Dryden adds here that he does not dispute the preference for tragedy generally felt in England. "But, 'tis unjust", he adds, "that they who have not the least notion of heroic writing should therefore condemn the pleasure which others receive from it, because they cannot comprehend it" (I, 199). His egalitarian judgement on this occasion is "let everyman enjoy his taste". Later, however, he does become more forthright in his preference. In both the *Discourse concerning ... Satire* (1693) and the Preface to the *Aeneid* (1697), epic is rated more highly: in the latter work his choice even entails an attack upon Aristotle's reasoning. Dryden remarks that

> it is one reason of Aristotle's to prove that tragedy is the more noble because it turns in a shorter compass ... He might prove as well that a mushroom is to be preferred before a peach, because it shoots up in the compass of a night.
> (II, 227)

This cleverly misplaces Aristotle's reason for arguing as he did. A peach presumably takes no longer to eat than a

---

[2] For convenience, all references are to *John Dryden: Of Dramatic Poesy, and Other Critical Essays*, ed. G. Watson (London, 1962). Here, I, 87.

[3] Cf. *Reflections*, II, 2; p.72.

mushroom, but a single tragedy would be much briefer in the performance than an entire epic. Now Aristotle argues precisely that "the more concentrated is much more pleasing than that diluted by a great length of time" (26.62b1-2). None the less, bearing in mind the temperate and reasonable nature of Dryden's criticism as well as its changeability, we would not want to agree with Thomas Twining's comment, elicited by the passage above, that Dryden's performance was determined by which genre he happened to have in sharper focus.[4]

Dryden's early acquaintance with Aristotle looks to be no more than a polite one. While, as we have seen, both Rymer and Dennis began their critical careers with a commitment to French Aristotelian criticism, Dryden's ties to it were more tenuous, and his link with the *Poetics* was correspondingly weaker. Indeed, the *Essay* displays inherited esteem for Aristotle rather than acquaintance with him. Dryden does advance some critical opinions that concern Aristotle at a distance. He says, for instance, that the rules were taken from the practice of classical writers, that Horace is a comment upon Aristotle, and that tragedies beget admiration, compassion, or concernment.[5] Even while holding, however, that the unity of place is not to be found deliberately observed in Greek tragedy, Dryden shows no awareness of Italian influence on the dramatic unities. He says that "we neither find it [the unity of place] in Aristotle, Horace, or any who have written of it [the theory of tragedy?], till in our age the French poets first made it a precept of the stage" (I, 36). Furthermore, there is strong evidence in the *Essay* that Dryden had only vague acquaintance with the technicalities of neo-classical criticism, particularly with its terminology. His quotation of Greek terms, for instance, is frequently marred by errors in precision and understanding. He cites both words that Aristotle uses for plot, but he gives to μῦθος a neuter gender

---

[4] Thus in *Aristotle's Treatise of Poetry, translated* (2nd edn, London, 1815), p. 396.

[5] See Watson, I, 27, 46.

instead of a masculine, and uses τῶν πραγμάτων σύνθεσις as though it meant the traditional material the poet handles ("only some tale derived from Thebes or Troy"), not the creative organisation of that material in a play (see I, 34). Further, when giving Aristotles phrase for the ridiculous in comedy, he repeats the definite article and talks of "the τὸ γελοῖον" (I, 72). Rather inconsistently, he does not fall into the same error a page or so later, when remarking that New Comedy tried to express "the ἦθος", where tragedy had expressed "the πάθος", of mankind. He leaves one wondering, therefore, whether it was ignorance, deference to the common solecism, or carelessness that led him to refer to the mob as "the ὁι πολλοί" (I, 86). More serious, however, than these errors of detail is the fact that Dryden attributes to Aristotle the division of a play into the four parts *protasis, casastasis, epitasis,* and *catastrophe* (I, 33). He cannot have a close familiarity with the contents of the *Poetics*, if he can make this attribution.

For the more general influence of the text of the *Essay* we do not have to go beyond the standing argument on whether or not rhyme is necessary in drama. "Crites" (the pseudonym in the *Essay* of Sir Robert Howard, who is its main supporter of the ancients) begins the discussion of rhyme by maintaining that

> it cannot be but unnatural to present the most free way of speaking in that which is the most constrained. For this reason, says Aristotle, 'tis best to write tragedy in that kind of verse ... which is nearest prose: and this amongst the Ancients was the iambic, and with us is blank verse. (I, 78-9)

Now Dryden is doing more here than make Howard side with the ancients, more than merely using Aristotle to give to Howard a convenient support for the position he is made to adopt. Howard had himself made the same point in his Preface to *Four New Plays* (1664):

> I believe that it may be concluded impossible that any should speak as good

John Dryden

verses in rhyme as the best poets have writ, and therefore that which seems nearest to what [dramatic writing] intends [i.e. extempore speech] is ever, ever to be preferred.[6]

Dryden's allusion to the doctrine of the *Poetics*, that the iambic is the basic metre of tragedy because it is "nearest everyday speech" (μάλιστα λεκτικόν, 4.49a24-5), is thus very apposite. Neither does the context of Aristotle's remark (which we may hazard Dryden knew little about) affect the application of it. However, Dryden's reply to Howard (I, 83-4) is less commendable. Margaret Sherwood writes as follows:

> Dryden [in the character of "Neander"] defends himself in upholding rime...by gravely proving that blank verse is "not a kind of verse", but only measured prose, and so fails to meet the Aristotelian demand; then by proving that couplet-verses may be rendered as near prose as blank verse itself--a species of argument in which he would hardly find a worthy antagonist.[7]

The evidence of the *Essay* suggests that it was fortunate that Dryden's knowledge of Aristotle improved. In addition to his attributing to Aristotle the extension made by J.C. Scaliger to the terminology Evanthius and Donatus employed in connection with Terentian comedy, there is the fact that he believes "neither Aristotle, nor Horace, nor any other who writ" on the subject of drama gave a definition of it (I, 25).

---

[6] *Dryden and Howard 1564-1668: The Text of "An Essay of Dramatic Poesy", "The Indian Emperor", and "The Duke of Lerma", with Other Controversial Matter*, ed. D. Arundel (Cambridge, 1929), p. 9.

[7] Margaret Sherwood, *Dryden's Dramatic Theory and Practice* (Boston, 1898), p. 27.

This indication of the distance at which the *Poetics* lay undermines Dryden's pretensions to touch on it. If he was capable of this remark (even after reading only commentators on Aristotle), then he was scarcely in a position to get anything right about the *Poetics*. One might argue in his defence that the occasion of his writing the *Essay* was, at least to begin with, an enforced retirement from London, so that while Aristotle was so much a part of common parlance that Dryden could not avoid reference to him, he may have had little chance to consult the appropriate sources. However, one would attach little weight to this speculation. It does not seem as though Dryden's references to the *Poetics* were forced on him: rather that he wished to show himself at home in all provinces of critical writing. Throughout his career, he is careful to give the impression of the sure touch, to which his title is not always sound. Perhaps, then, the general distaste of his age for minute scholarship explains his frequent carelessness--though one must add that, if Dryden had been writing on, for instance, the Jeremy Collier stage controversy, he would have been torn to shreds on just this count.

With the *Heads of an Answer to Rymer* the position changes considerably. Dryden puts down his thoughts on Rymer's *Tragedies of the Last Age* in the end papers of the copy Rymer sent him. He offered a sustained challenge to Rymer's arguments and to the classical authority behind them. Potentially at least (the work was never published), the *Heads* was by far the most damning of Dryden's criticisms of Aristotle. Rymer had both argued the superiority of the Ancients and brought the doctrine of poetic justice into some popularity in England. Dryden tackles him on each count. At least in the early sections, Dryden bases his attack on the proposition that pity and fear, the emotions to which Greek tragedy was taken to be confined, do not really give enough scope to the dramatist. It needs to be recognised, he says, that in tragedy

> not only pity and terror are to be moved as the only means to bring us to virtue, but generally love to virtue and hatred to vice; by shewing the rewards of one, and punishments of the other; at least by

rendering virtue always amiable, though it be
unfortunate; and vice detestable, tho' it be
shown triumphant. If then the encouragement
of virtue and discouragement of vice be the
proper ends of poetry in tragedy: pity and
terror, tho' good means, are not the only. For
all the passions in their turns are to be set in a
ferment. (I, 213)

Dryden further specifies the range of emotions he would like the dramatist to have open to him:

If terror and pity are only to be raised,
certainly [Rymer] follows Aristotle's rules,
and Sophocles's and Euripides's example; but
joy may be raised too, and that doubly, either
by seeing a wicked man punished, or a good
man at last fortunate; or perhaps indignation,
to see wickedness prosperous and goodness
depressed: both these may be profitable to the
end of tragedy, reformation of manners; but
the last improperly, only as it begets pity in
the audience: tho' Aristotle, I confess, places
tragedies of this kind in the second form.
(I, 217-18)

All this is by no means as clear as it might be. Having appeared to challenge the critical standpoint that grounds poetic justice in the *Poetics* (by linking poetic justice with supposedly new emotions), Dryden suddenly accepts the jurisdiction of Aristotle. His new development, which purports to allow for tragedies of indignation, in fact allows only for pity. Furthermore, "tragedies of this kind" (which I take to be tragedies of indignation) are subjected to Aristotle's disapproval. Dryden seems to have given his case away, even in the process of presenting it. This may be because he recognises the difficulty of limiting the ancients so severely. We may, in other words, have felt in reading both sections that the mutual exclusiveness implied between the emotions of pity and fear and poetic justice was not really legitimate. Our uneasiness is justified when he makes the following qualification:

> And if after all, in a larger sense, pity comprehends this concernment for the good, and terror includes detestation for the bad, then let us consider whether the English have not answered this end of tragedy as well as the Ancients, or perhaps better.
>
> (I, 213)

Having thus changed his point of attack, Dryden would have done well to give more emphasis than he did to a perceptive point made in connection with *Rollo*. Allowing for poetic justice to be felt in tragedies of indignation as well as in tragedies of joy, he observes:

> we stab [the villain] in our minds for every offence which he commits; the point which the poet is to gain on the audience is not so much in the death of an offender, as the raising an horror of his crimes.
>
> (I, 215)

If Dryden had gone to any lengths in extending this perception into a principle, then it might have struck at the very roots of rigid formalist prescription in this field. It would certainly have offered a challenge to the most basic of the principle's main underlying theory--the out-and-out condemnation of the portrayal of any successful villain (13.52b36). However, no development is offered of this point, and the implicit challenge to the absolute position that allowed only for tragedies of joy was not made explicit in any later work.

The principal remaining topic of the *Heads* is that of the relative importance of the parts of drama. For Aristotle there were six parts (plot, character, diction, thought, spectacle, and song--6.50a9-10), and plot was unequivocally the most important (6.50a15). Many in Dryden's age emphasised character at the expense of plot; Dryden however, gave much greater importance to diction. He suggests, on his own behalf I think, that plot should be made primary only in a technical and logical sense, though it is not impossible that he thought this was really Aristotle's own intention. The antithesis between "his" and "ours" in the following passage suggests, however, that the former is the more likely interpretation: accordingly, I shall interpolate words to suggest that the opinion expressed is Dryden's own. The answer to Rymer, he says,

> ought to prove ... that the fable is not the greatest masterpiece of a tragedy, tho' it be the foundation of it ... Aristotle places the fable first; [and it should be, but] not *quoad dignitatem, sed quoad fundamentum*; for a fable, never so movingly contrived to those ends of his, pity and terror, will operate nothing on our affections, except the characters, manners, thoughts, and words are suitable. (I, 211)

Dryden's reason for qualifying the importance given to plot becomes further apparent in a later section: he comments that Rapin

> attributes more to the *dictio*, that is, to the words and discourses of a tragedy, than Aristotle had done, who places them in the last rank of beauties; perhaps [we should make them] only last in order, because they are the last product of the design, of the disposition or connection of its parts. (I, 219)

I think we need a little more evidence before we can say that for Dryden plot and diction keep their traditional places when considered technically, but reverse them when considered as "beauties". The position is, as yet, rather ambiguous, since I have merely put what I consider the most likely interpretation on his words. Fortunately, we can turn for further evidence to Charles Gildon's *Complete Art of Poetry* (1718), where it is remarked that

> Mr. Dryden ... in more places than one, seems to place the excellence of a Play in the

> Language, and not in the *Plot*; particularly in a Copy of Verses of his to Mr. *Southern*, where he has this Line: *So Terence plotted, but so Terence writ*: by which he plainly gives the Preference to the Language of *Terence*.
>
> (I, 223)[8]

It seems clear, then, that Dryden made an isolated attempt to controvert Aristotle on the importance of the parts. Had the *Heads* been published, others who felt discomfort at the prominence given to plot might have been glad to gain Dryden's support here. Dryden himself shows something of the more common tendency, when he comments adversely in the *Essay of Dramatic Poesy* (I, 34) on the worn-out plots of which the "talkative Greeklings" were so fond.[9] He implies not only that the plots of the Greeks were too limited in scope, but that the emphasis on plot itself is itself too constricting.

Turning again to the *Heads*, we may also note that Dryden could not there reply to Rymer's most damning critique of Shakespeare--that was not to appear until *A Short View*, with its analysis of *Othello*. Even so, Dryden does base part of his reply to Rymer on the particular examples of Shakespeare and Fletcher, while examining the principles in which modern drama differs from the ancient. He writes that "the dispositions of the people to whom a poet writes, may be so different that what pleased the Greeks would not satisfy an English audience" (I, 214). We are justified, then,

---

[8] Gildon quotes "To Mr. Southern, on his Comedy called The Wives Excuse", line 15.

[9] Dryden cites Ben Jonson for the phrase, for which editors quote *Discoveries*: "which of the Greeklings ever durst give precept to *Demosthenes*" (*Works*, ed. Herford and Simpson, VIII (Oxford, 1947), p. 641), which does not very well fit the context. One could as easily cite two neighbouring passages: "*Demaratus* ... answered ... too much talking is ever the *Indice* of a foole", or "*Zeno* ... replyed ... talking is the disease of Age".

in assuming that Dryden was facing a practical problem. The English drama placed its emphasis elsewhere than on plot, and if theory was to come into line with practice, then something had to be done about Aristotle's emphasis on it. Not only is the fable "in the English more adorned with episodes, and larger than in the Greek poets; consequently more diverting" (I, 215-16), but the diction and the manners of English drama make a greater demand on the attention than the Aristotelian scheme, strictly applied, will allow for. When the relative status of all the parts was under consideration, as it was in the *Heads*, the conflict between Aristotelian theory and English practice was more strongly felt. It is thus again regrettable that Dryden did not carry his analysis further. If he had, two areas in the critical thought of his time might have been given a new and more vibrant tone.

In addition to the two main points of principle with which the *Heads* is involved, there is one matter of detail to which the *Poetics* is directly relevant. In commenting on a difficulty in understanding Rymer's argument in *A Short View*, Dryden points (I, 219) to one "obscurity" (as he calls it)

> where he says Sophocles perfected tragedy by introducing the third actor; that is, he meant three kinds of action, one company singing or speaking, another playing on the music, a third dancing.

Here we need to recognise that, when he read him, Dryden must have seen that Rymer was making that use of the *Poetics*. Rymer had said that "*Sophocles* adding a *third* Actor, and *painted* Scenes, gave (in *Aristotle*'s opinion) the utmost perfection to tragedy" (Zimansky, p. 22). Therefore, if Dryden thought that Rymer was obscure, reference to the *Poetics* might easily have cleared the matter up for him. He might, to be sure, have still entertained the strange notion that "actor" meant "kind of action", but he could hardly have continued to believe that Sophocles made innovations of the kind he suggested, when he read that Aeschylus increased the number of actors from one to two and *decreased* the part played by the chorus (see 4.49a17). Perhaps Dryden's fuller working of the notes that constitute the *Heads* as it stands would have made all clear. The Preface to *Troilus and Cressida* (1679), containing "The Grounds of Criticism in Tragedy", represents a fuller working of some of the ideas in the *Heads*. It is, however, a much less forceful work, and the criticisms of the *Poetics* are severely retrenched. Dryden had gone so far in the *Heads* as to say that if Aristotle had seen the writing of later times, he might well have changed his mind on certain important critical matters (I, 218). Now he remarks that

> If any one will ask me whether a tragedy cannot be made upon any other grounds than those of exciting pity and terror in us, Bossu, the best of modern critics, answers thus in general: that all excellent arts, and particularly that of poetry, have been invented and brought to perfection by men of a transcendent genius; and that therefore they who practice afterwards the same arts are obliged to tread in their footsteps, and to search in their writings the foundation of them. (I, 246)

This exhibits a greater conservatism than we would normally attribute to Dryden, but the view is one that colours his longest published encounter with the *Poetics*, and makes that encounter relatively unimportant for our purposes. There is little in it that is either original or detailed, where the *Poetics* is concerned. Furthermore, all the incipient lines of attack detectable in the *Heads* have been closed. Even the special attention said to be due to Shakespeare and Fletcher, from which much of the liberalising impulse of the earlier work had stemmed, is now subjected to limitations: "we ought to follow them so far only as they have copied the excellencies of those who invented and brought to perfection dramatic poetry" (I, 246).

Opinion in the neo-classical period was divided on this point. Some thought Shakespeare's native genius raised him to the level that other poets could achieve only by observation of the rules: others thought his plays could be mended by observing them. Dryden, whose more normal critical attitude to Shakespeare might perhaps have been that his genius was indeed enough, is here writing a preface to a

John Dryden

regularisation of *Troilus and Cressida*. His conservatism may thus be explained as a piece of special pleading, or at least as being condition by the corrective task he had undertaken.

The Preface also contains Dryden's nearest attempt at emendation of the *Poetics*, though, his proposed change of reading is designed to bring the *Poetics* into line with his own ideas. While, at one point, objecting to rant in drama, he writes as follows:

> They who would justify the madness of poetry from the authority of Aristotle have mistaken the text, and consequently the interpretation: I imagine it to be false read, where he says of poetry that it is εὐφυοῦς ἢ μανικοῦ, that it had always somewhat in it either of a genius or of a madman. 'Tis more probable that the original ran thus, that poetry was ἐυφυοῦς οὐ μανικοῦ, that it belongs to a witty man, but not to a madman.   (I, 255)

Dryden enjoins the poet, with Le Bossu (III, ix), to warm his audience by degrees, so that actor and audience work up to a pitch together. Now, in making the point he employs a favourite neo-classical device, that of being wittily sarcastic at the expense of bombast, and he gives a fine example of the technique in a criticism of the Hecuba speech in *Hamlet* (see I, 257-8). While in this mood, Dryden comes to Aristotle and proposes his emendation.

The first modern edition to agree with Dryden's proposition was actually the most radical of them. Else translates the passage as follows:

> These are the reasons why the poetic art is an enterprise for the gifted (rather than) the "manic" individual.   (p. 486)

Else points out that Aristotle's sentence begins with "διό", a word that puts us on our guard to catch the sequence of thought. He comments that "the preceding sentence is a long and complex one, including adjurations to (1) visualize the action, the whereabouts of the characters, etc., and (2) incorporate their expressions of feeling in appropriate figures". It is evident that "what is required of the poet above all is *readiness of mind, keen observation, and adaptability* to an almost infinite variety of human situations" (p. 496). Else thus concludes (in the light of Aristotle's attitude elsewhere to μανία, which suggests it is essentially a deviation) that the poet can scarcely be said to be capable of the kind of control he needs over his medium, if he is subject to the kind of mental disturbance μανία implies. Other modern editions had not taken Else's line, largely because it was considered that μανία is Aristotle's equivalent for the Platonic *furor poeticus*. Butcher had thus translated μανικός by the words "strain of madness",[10] and Bywater by "a touch of madness" (p. 49). Else points out, however, that against the numerous passages in Aristotle where μανία must imply a mental disturbance or deviation greater than "a strain" implies, there are only very few where Plato's "frenzied rapture" might be echoed (see p. 497). As so often, the matter cannot be said to be conclusive: none the less, Else adduced a good deal of evidence in favour of his view.

More importantly for us, it coincides with the kind of attitude that Dryden wishes us to adopt. Dryden's attention was probably turned to this part of the *Poetics* by Rapin, and neither critic really does justice to the possibilities of the text. Rymer translates Rapin as follows: "*Aristotle* allows that there is something Divine in [the poet's] character, but nothing of Madness" (I, v, p. 6). Dryden, on the other hand, translated ἐυφυοῦς by "witty", where Rymer had offered "Divine". Both writers thus make it very difficult, if not impossible, for μανικός to be taken as an equivalent for ἐνθέος and to be translated as "divinely inspired". The possible echo of Plato is not allowed to come through at all, and, in this context at least, Dryden was not of the opinion that "Great Wits are sure to Madness near ally'd" (*Absalom and Achitophel*, line 163). His emendation accords with his definition of "wit" as "a propriety of thoughts and words" (I,

---

[10] Thus in *Aristotle's Theory of Poetry and Fine Art* (4th edn, New York, 1951), p. 53.

207) and with his contention that the third happiness of a poet's imagination, elocution, is the art of clothing thought in "apt, significant, and sounding words" (I, 98).

We come now to two more general principles in Dryden's criticism to which Aristotle is pertinent. One concerns the pleasures of imitation, the other the vital concept of unity. On the former topic *A Parallel betwixt Painting and Poetry* (1695) challenges the *Poetics* in the following terms:

> Aristotle tells us that imitation pleases, because it affords matter for a reasoner to inquire into the truth or falsehood of imitation, by comparing its likeness, or unlikeness, with the original. But by this rule, every speculation in nature whose truth falls under the inquiry of a philosopher, must produce the same delight which is not true. I should rather assign another reason. Truth is the object of our understanding, as good is of our will; and the understanding can no more be delighted with a lie than the will can choose an apparent evil. As truth is the end of our speculations, so the discovery of it is the pleasure of them; and since a true knowledge of nature gives us pleasure, a lively imitation of it, either in poetry or painting, must of necessity produce a much greater. (II, 193-4)

Here again we need to have recourse to Dacier as well as to Aristotle, before we can deal with the passage in hand. As Twining asserted in answer to Dryden, Aristotle proposes, in chapter IV, a truth "for the generality of mankind", not solely for the φιλοσόφοι.[11] But where Aristotle remarked that men enjoy imitation, "because they learn and reason on each thing" (4.48b15-17), Dacier commented that imitation "gives to the Mind an occasion of reasoning, and making reflexions, insomuch that it always apprehends something

---

[11] Twining, p. 152.

new" (Remarks, IV 6, p. 37). It was not difficult for Dryden then to take it upon himself and say that Aristotle attributes the pleasure taken in imitation to the opportunity it presents of detecting truth or falsehood in the imitation. He could extend the argument as he understood it, and suggest the view it entailed did not allow for degrees in the pleasure experienced.The opportunity, he argues, to consider whether or not an imitation be true or false is not enough to cause pleasure--it needs to *be* true.

All this, I think, is just to Aristotle--even though Dryden's conception of what he says is remote. The point of Aristotle's remark, which has not been lost, is that pleasure comes to man because he learns, and the learning itself is what causes the pleasure (4.48b9, 13). Dryden, then, has not distorted Aristotle, even though he does not know exactly what he says. He merely differs with him. The theory of learning that lies behind chapter IV determines that the opportunity to learn is, for Aristotle, pleasing in itself. For Dryden the discovery of truth is what causes the pleasure. His sophistication of Aristotle has much to do with what we shall later find replaced the philosophical background of chapter IV. Though Dryden disagreed with Aristotle on this last point, he was none the less much attracted to the emphasis the *Poetics* gave to the role of intelligence and intelligibility in art. However, if we examine the passages of the *Poetics* that deal with this matter, we find that one very important aspect of unity is passed over by the neo-classicists, Dryden being no exception. It was either the subjective or else the technical aspect of unity that appealed to them--its organic aspect was disregarded. Dryden writes, for instance, that

> Aristotle commends the unity of action in a poem, because the mind is not capable of digesting many things at once, nor of conceiving fully any more than one idea at a time ... Now unity, which is defined, is in its nature more apt to be understood than multiplicity, which in some measure participates of infinity.   (II, 8)

With this remark we should compare *Poetics*, 8.51a16-18: "A plot is not one, as some think, because it is about one man; for an infinite variety of things happen to one man, from which (some of them) no unity can be made". The appeal of this kind of remark comes to the neo-classicists from the fact that they felt so strongly the necessity for order and logic in writing. The most obvious corollary, technically speaking, to the principle of unity thus understood was the job of giving a play one single focal point. Tragi-comedy and double plots were either inexcusable, or allowable only when the strands were woven so artfully together that the knot they formed could be cut with one stroke. Dryden himself sometimes supported double plots, sometimes condemned them, and sometimes argued for their justification. But, while he did tend to vary his principle with his practice--on one occasion he "broke a rule for the pleasure of variety" (I, 279), on another he condemned what he had done (II, 202), and on two occasions argued for local taste (II, 49, 161)--at no time did he offer a challenge to the principle of orderly representation.

While, then, Aristotle was thoroughly acceptable where the good sense that came from logical order was at issue, far less attention was paid to what, in the *Poetics*, is an equally important facet of unity. A work of art gains a kind of natural autonomy and organic independence, in Aristotle's eyes, from the properties of order and arrangement inherent in beauty. Furthermore, just as a visible object must be εὐσύνοπτον, "easily taken in by the eye", if it is to appear beautiful, the plot of a tragedy must be εὐμνημόνευτον, "easily retained by the memory", if it is to have any success. In this respect the principles of art work when they copy the laws of nature (an idea that does *not* appear in so many words in the *Poetics*). Butcher says, quite rightly, that "as a biological law [the principle of size] applies to the healthy life and growth of all organic structures. It is also an artistic law, expressing one of the first conditions of organic beauty" (pp. 276-7). On this principle one would find it hard not to describe Sir Richard Blackmore's epics as dinosaurs.

I think it possible to account for the lack of attention given to this aspect of the *Poetics* by reference not only to the critical tradition under which it was subsumed, but also to that "pious sagacity" common in neo-classical critical writing. The humane speculation in which the critics of the period frequently indulged in critical contexts, we have just seen Dryden exercise on the topic of the pleasures of imitation. Now, the Horatian tradition of criticism concentrated its attention largely on the relation between poet and audience: the *Poetics*, on the other hand, gives at least an equal importance to the relation between poet and the work of art. But of course the influence of moral speculation in neo-classical writing is pervasive, affecting far more than just poetic theory. For instance, just as the neo-classicist ignores the organic aspect of art, so also he tends to see past the organic aspect of nature. Where Aristotle's theory of poetry extends the laws of nature into those of art, the neo-classicist views both fields with an improving eye. We find that Addison, for instance, expresses some rapture, in *Spectator*, no. 353, at the pleasure the eye may take in nature, and he remarks that this pleasure will raise a "rational Admiration in the Soul". But the brooks, woods, and fields call up in him a purely subjective reaction to their murmurs, shades and embroidery, a reaction that leads him to pious reflections on the Supreme Cause that regulates nature. His dutiful regard to the regularity that proclaims its Great Original (which sanctions his inclusion in the hymn books) determines that he invest nature with no autonomy and no structure of its own. Nature is ordered, but has no significant organic autonomy.

    It seems to me arguable that the autonomy withheld from nature is also withheld from art, and that this is evident in the imagery the neo-classicists use to express the unity of art. Aristotle maintains that a work of art should be like a single whole creature (23.59a 20; 7.50b34ff.). But Johnson complains of *Samson Agonistes* in terms that suggest order is to be imposed from without. There is, he says, no "regular and unbroken concatenation" of events in the play (*Rambler*, no. 139). Rymer, too, thought in the same terms, when he said, of a hypothetical modern analogy for the *Persae*, that it should take place at the Louvre, "for there the Tragedy wou'd principally operate, and there the Lines most naturally centre" (Zimansky, p. 91). Finally, Dryden himself remarks that "as in perspective, so in tragedy, there must be a point of sight in which all the lines terminate; otherwise the eye wanders, and the work is false" (I, 244).

The visual and linear imagery of the English critics is perhaps motivated by their insistent desire for intelligibility, which itself makes for a rhetorical bias in the instructions given to the poet. There is no reflection, in them, of Aristotle's prior emphasis on the natural properties inherent in art.

On the question of how the poet is to represent men, two passages spring to mind from the *Poetics*. In the first it is remarked that men will be shown to be either better, worse, or the same as we are, and to this extent the poet will copy what has been the practice of the painter. Polygnotus, for instance, made men better, Pauson worse, Dionysius the same (2.48a1-6). Here the ideal, the pessimistic, and the realist modes of representation are suggested. Much later, however, the poet is allowed to be excused from censure, if his representation is either ideal, or actual, or in accordance with tradition. Sophocles, says Aristotle, maintained that his portrait was of man as he should be, where Euripides' was of man as he is. If neither defence will satisfy, Aristotle continues, then perhaps the portrait accords with tradition (see 25.50b31-5). Now Rapin referred to this latter passage, but only to the section that mentioned Sophocles and Euripides, and he made Aristotle express a preference. He thought that "*Sophocles*, who in his *Tragedies* represents men as they *ought* to be, is, in the opinion of Aristotle, to be prefer'd before *Euripides*, who represents Men as really they *are*" (*Reflections*, I, xxiv, p. 35). When Dryden ventured into this area, the confusion only increased:

> Sophocles, says Aristotle, always drew men as they ought to be, that is better than they were: another, whose name I have forgotten, drew them worse than naturally they were. Euripides altered nothing in the character, but made them such as they were represented by history, epic poetry, or tradition. Of the three, the draught of Sophocles is most commended by Aristotle.
> (II, 202)

It is impossible to say how Dryden arrived at this view, but his tone implies that he may be excused the labour of finding out who the third poet was--his memory for names is a little hazy, but the facts are there, he suggests. Even so, he gives an impression of confidence that he has little title to assume.

There are times when Dryden's imprecision may be referred to the general distaste of his times for close scholarship: if the prop of classical authority is taken away, there is still good sense left to support the critical idea advanced. It is just this indifference that is reflected in Dryden: it is true that he maintains, in the *Defence of An Essay of Dramatic Poesy* (1688), that he has a "veneration for Aristotle, Horace, Ben Johnson [sic] and Corneille" that will not allow him to side with Howard. But this says no more than that Howard flies in the face of these venerable critics; not that Dryden would not be above doing so.

A passage more typical of him is to be found in the Preface to *All for Love*, where he prefers his own opinion, "till some genius as universal as Aristotle shall arise" (I, 225). This attitude allows for a mutual independence to exist It is also mid-way between the extremes he adopts. In the *Heads*, Dryden thought that "'tis not enough that Aristotle has said so, for Aristotle drew his models of tragedy from Sophocles and Euripides; and if he had seen ours, might have changed his mind" (I, 216). But the sharpness of this attack is to be countered by the complete conservatism of "The Grounds of Criticism in Tragedy". On this later occasion Dryden wants common and undisputed ground, the best perspective he could find for his readers to judge his regularising of *Troilus and Cressida*. Twining, who was on the watch for the way Dryden treated Aristotle, remarked that he appeared to have taken his idea of him from the French (see p. 396), scarcely ever mentioning him without finding "that he looked only at the wrong side of the tapestry" (p. 152). But I think we should conclude that, while Dryden certainly was not accurate in his handling of the text, it was a matter of temperament with him to use rather than merely to import critical ideas. Sometimes Aristotle provided a useful, because widely accepted, view from which he could dissent in a carefully tempered and reasonable way, and sometimes a measured conformity was more advantageous. In both cases Dryden built upon him to his own satisfaction.

CHAPTER FOUR: POETIC JUSTICE

When Rymer first gave full expression to the doctrine of poetic justice into England (for there had been some sketchy earlier treatment of it in English criticism),[1] his leading principle was that the poet had a duty to observe "that necessary relation and chain, whereby the causes and the effects, the vertues and rewards, the vices and their punishments are proportion'd and link'd together" (Zimansky, p. 75). He left the working out of the system to be elaborated from this basic requirement to men "of more flegm and consideration" (ibid.), and the qualifications and riders grew to be legion. He did, however, give a lead to some critics, when he attributed the practice of the doctrine to the Greek dramatists.[2] So, also, when he emphasised that poetic justice should be seen to have been done--the spectator must not have to "trust the *Poet* for a *Hell* behind the *Scenes* " (p. 27).

From the wealth of criticism that followed Rymer's meagre beginnings, I wish to give attention to the two main factors--ἀμαρτία and endings--that relate directly to the *Poetics*. Both factors, of course, entail the stipulations that Aristotle laid down for the character of the protagonist, and I shall begin with these, giving attention to the fact that the formalists understood ἀμαρτία to have moral connotations. I shall then pass to the question of endings, basing my discussion on the differences of opinion expressed by Dennis and Addison on the subject.

While it was often stated by the formalists that good must be rewarded and evil punished in drama, there was also an embargo on the creation of merely good characters who were given their due, and evil ones who where consigned to punishment. The *Poetics* may well have been influential on this point: Aristotle did not even consider the case of the

---

[1] Hooker I, 437 mentions Sidney and Jonson, but only as "foreshadowing" and as "approaching" the idea.

[2] So also does Temple's *Of Poetry* (1690) and Blackmore's Preface to *Prince Arthur* (1695).

good man subjected to no trials and rewarded for his virtue. And Dryden, in a moment of candour, maintained on his own behalf that "as for a perfect character of virtue, it never was in nature, and therefore there can be no imitation of it" (I, 246). Perhaps not all critics would have echoed Dryden's unflinching view of human nature, but by one route or another (and largely for elementary dramatic reasons) they did arrive at the position where at least some trial was to be made of virtue. Not a few found the position decided for them by Aristotle, when he determined that the man with mixed qualities should be the protagonist (see 13.53a7). But, even while accepting this requirement as essential, the formalist was still not in a position to assume the automatic operation of "the relation and chain" that Rymer had proposed. It was also necessary to regard Aristotle's ἁμαρτία as specifically a moral failing. It was only when this interpretation had been made that the hero could be burdened with that culpability which would justify his being punished.

To see how essential this further specification was, we may take a look at the case James Drake made against taking ἁμαρτία in the sense required. There was, we shall find, at least one critic in the neo-classical period who could argue not only persuasively and sanely, but also with justice to the *Poetics*, that Aristotle does not support poetic justice. *The Ancient and Modern Stages Survey'd* (1699) was written in answer to Jeremy Collier's *Short View of the Immorality and Profaneness of the English Stage* (1698). In it Drake is not concerned to condemn poetic justice, but rather to appropriate the device to the moderns. Naturally, part of his case rests on the evidence of Greek drama, as well as on the picture of it that the *Poetics* affords. His overall interpretation of Greek tragedy leads him to the conclusion that it was not concerned to inculcate a moral, as was so often assumed by his age. In fact he argues that since

> we find few *Moral* Plays amongst the remains of those extraordinary Persons the *Greek* Tragedians, we may fairly presume, that they did not take at *Athens*, otherwise they wou'd have been more cultivated. For this reason

probably it was, that *Aristotle* took so slender notice of Moral Tragedy, as not thinking it worth while to lay down rules for the practice of that, which was no longer in use, or esteem, amongst his Countrymen in his Time
(pp. 224- 5)

Aristotle's mention of "moral" tragedy is slender indeed, and consists solely of two examples--the *Phthiotides* and the *Peleus* (see 18.56a1-2), of which nothing illuminating is known. However, the effect of Drake's interpretation of Greek tragedy reaches much further. By it, he is led to conclude that Aristotle recommends "the misfortunes of a Person unhappy thro his mistake not his Fault, as the most proper Subject for Tragedy" (pp. 226-7).

Now any formalist who read this could not have failed to see that it put the whole doctrine of poetic justice in jeopardy, as far as grounding it in the *Poetics* was concerned. The standard view was that the passions of the hero had to lead him into error, and that it was this error that allowed him to be punished. But Drake, with something of our modern notion of what ἁμαρτία is, maintains that Aristotle did *not* make the heroes' "proper Demerits the Standard, or immediate rule for Squaring their future Fortune" (p. 227). Thus Drake can agree with Dryden that "the good which is in [the chief persons] shall outweigh the bad", but he cannot further agree that this imbalance allows (at least in Greek tragedy and on the authority of Aristotle) "room for punishment on the one side, and pity on the other" (Watson, I, 246). What punishment there is can be inflicted, on Drake's terms, only for "proper Demerits".

In a fuller analysis Drake would have found time to elaborate his opinion as to what should happen to an Oedipus. As it is, he merely comments that "*Moral* Tragedy not admitting such Incidents as were proper to move Terror or Compassion, the Springs of Passion were wanting, and consequently the Audience were but weakly affected" (p. 225). But certainly Drake is not obliged, as Dacier was (*Remarks*, XIII, 11), to show that Oedipus deserved to be driven to tearing his eyes out.

So far Drake has stated a case without arguing for a reinterpretation of Greek drama to replace the traditional one. When he does offer his explanation of why Greek tragedy did not observe poetic justice, he points to the nature of its subject-matter. This, he says, was traditional: the Greek tragedians were "more solicitous to make their stories conform to the relation, or to the publick Opinion, than to Poetick Justice" (p. 229). Thus, he feels, "by this means all hopes of a *Moral* was cut off, or if by chance the story afforded any, we are more obliged to the Poets luck for it, than his Skill or Care" (ibid.).

A comparison of what different Greek dramatists made of the same myth shows this conclusion to be greatly overstated. But none the less it would be unfair to deny Drake his position altogether. He has erred to one side, where his age tended to err equally on the other. Thus, as long as the formalist can say that Aristotle allows the poet to defend his portrait of life from an idealist position (25.60b10), Drake may be allowed to assert that he also allows the traditionalist position. Furthermore, there is truth in his observation that the morality in Greek drama tends to be located in "wise sayings, scattered here and there up and down the Dialogue" (p. 191).

He points out, too, that even *Oedipus Tyrannus*, "noble and beautiful to admiration, for the Structure and Contrivance of it, is yet very deficient in the Moral". It contains "nothing in it but a lazy, unactive speculation" (pp. 131-2). Making some allowance for the forcefulness put upon him by the occasion of his writing (his answering Jeremy Collier), we may feel inclined to support Drake, and recognise that the *Oedipus Tyrannus* does indeed conclude with the maxim that we should count no man happy until he dies.

As I have already hinted, Drake did not give much attention to the matter of endings, except where he implied that they should be unfortunate--the hero is to be "unhappy" through his fault. For this topic, we turn to Addison and Dennis. In April, 1711, Addison wrote two consecutive papers for the *Spectator* in which the doctrine of poetic justice was subjected to no little scorn. Addison provoked Dennis considerably by maintaining that it was a ridiculous modern doctrine, of whose origin he archly declared he was ignorant. The poet, he thought, had to realise that Fortune treats all men alike, which made it ridiculous for him to set himself up as a mimic dispenser of Divine Retribution. Indeed, Seneca put the matter admirably when he said that "a Virtuous Man ... strugling with Misfortunes, is such a Spectacle as Gods might look upon with Pleasure".[3]

In these early papers, then, the effect of tragedy, for Addison, is to promote speculative edification, not to give instruction in morals. Tragedy must "wear out of our Thoughts every thing that is mean and little" (I, 164), and the notion that a virtuous man absolutely must be delivered from his ill fortune "has no Foundation in Nature, in Reason, or in the Practice of the Ancients" (I, 169).

We should note, however, that Addison's view is not as purely theoretic as these quotations suggest. There is evidence in these papers that his real concern is with a practical situation. Paper no. 40 opens as follows:

> The *English* Writers of Tragedy are possessed with a Notion, that when they represent a virtuous or innocent Person in Distress, they ought not to leave him till they have delivered him out of his Troubles, or made him triumph over his Enemies. (I, 168)

Now from what Addison says later in this essay, some emphasis should be placed on "*English* ". The automatic observance of poetic justice, Addison continues, "would very much cramp the *English* Tragedy, and perhaps give a wrong Bent to the Genius of our Writers" (I, 170). Addison's target is not only "the Criticism that would establish [poetic justice] as the only Method" of writing, but also the criticism that fails to see that the Greek tragedians "by making Virtue sometimes happy and sometimes miserable, as they found it in the Fable which they made choice of", in effect "treated Men in their Plays, as they are dealt with in the World" (I, 169).

---

[3] All references to *The Spectator*, ed. D.F. Bond (5 vols, Oxford, 1965): the above reference is to I, 163-4.

Addison thus complements Drake's case admirably. The taunt at those, who, like Dennis, were inflexible in their advocacy of poetic justice is neatly combined with a concern for an actual situation. Dennis would have been unlikely to accept Addison's terms, even if he had seen the concern they expressed. He found it necessary to reply ironically to the "insolent and dogmatick" air of the article (no. 40) by pointing out that

> The first who establish'd this ridiculous Doctrine of modern Criticism, was a Certain modern Critick, who liv'd above two thousand Years ago; and who tells us expresly in the thirteenth Chapter of his critical *Spectator*, which Pedants call his Poetick ... *that we must not choose a very good Man, to plunge him from a prosperous Condition into Adversity*.[4]

Beneath Dennis's sarcasm lies a characteristic seriousness and forcefulness. For him the whole rationale of tragedy involves poetic justice. Without the moral there was no point in having the fable; and the poet has the explicit duty, as he says elsewhere, of ensuring that "the Good must never fail to prosper, and the Bad must be always punish'd" (II, 6).

The justification for drawing Aristotle into the debate lies, also, in Dennis's view, in the fact that he advocates the kind of happy ending to a play that will make for the distribution of reward and punishment. At another point in chapter XIII, there is according to Dennis "a very formal Recommendation of the impartial and exact Execution of poetical Justice" (II, 19). But even a cursory examination of the passage alluded to reveals that this is an overstatement amounting to serious misrepresentation. Aristotle remarks that "the finest tragedy, technically speaking, is formed upon this construction", i.e. where there is "a change of fortune, not from bad to good, but from good to bad, because of some great mistake" (13.53a13-16). The other, and the only

---

[4] *To the Spectator, Upon his Paper on the 16th of April*, in Hooker, II, 19.

other, alternative presented is that which Dennis calls Aristotle's "second Preference". It constitutes in fact a relegation to a firmly subordinate position of "that which is spoken of by some as the first: it has a double ending, as does the *Odyssey*, and finishes in opposites for the good and the bad" (a30-3). It can be seen, then, that Dennis is entitled to no more here than the claim that Aristotle takes note of the alternative he wishes to be favoured: he cannot properly assert that Aristotle recommends it in any way.

That Addison does not rest his case on classical authority appears the more fortunate when we do see him turn his attention to the *Poetics*. In *Spectator*, no. 273 (12 January 1712). Addison offers what appears to be intrinsically a quite acceptable series of statements: but as a representation of Aristotle, they leave much to be desired. He gives his own version of

> an admirable Observation out of *Aristotle*, which hath been very much misrepresented in the Quotations of some Modern Criticks. "If a Man of perfect and consummate Virtue falls into a Misfortune, it raises our Pity, but not our Terror, because we do not fear it may be our own Case, who do not resemble the Suffering person." But as that great Philosopher adds, "If we see a Man of virtue mixt with Infirmities, fall into any Misfortune, it does not only raise our Pity but our Terror; because we are afraid the like Misfortunes may happen to our selves, who resemble the Character of the Suffering Person."
>
> (II, 565-6)

A reader with any faith in Addison's quotation marks would be sadly disillusioned if he turned to a text of the *Poetics*. He would, for one thing, discover that Addison has designated pitiable a situation that Aristotle brands as morally offensive.

We need something of the context here: with it present in our minds, we will find that the distance between Addison and his source will seem immense--far greater than the reasonableness of what he says would suggest. The actual words that Addison purports to quote translate as follows: "Nor must the poet show good men falling from good fortune into bad, for this is neither fearful, nor pitiable, but morally offensive ... The intermediate person, then, is left--he who is not distinguished for virtue and justice, and who is brought into misfortune, not by evil and depravity, but by some error of judgment" (13.52b34-6; 53a7-10).

The first half of this passage is our immediate concern. In it Aristotle uses, by extension, a word that carries the sense of the highest degree of guilt and uncleanness, a pollution that would debar its victim from all rights of access in the community. In tragedy the word covers a situation in which pity and fear pale by comparison with the moral shock administered. Now luckily the word appears again in a later passage of the *Poetics*, where its function in Aristotle's criticism is made much clearer. At 14.53b37 ff., Aristotle indicates that, of two situations where murder is contemplated in tragedy, that one is μιαρόν in which the deed is *not done* : it is both μιαρόν and non-tragic.

As Else pointed out (p. 422), the two terms work independently of one another and correspond to the two main characteristics of the situation they describe. "To be about to kill" is μιαρόν--even when the deed is not done. "Not to do the deed" is non-tragic, because there is no "painful or destructive action" (11.52b11-12). Nor if the deed is done. There is still pollution, but the act begins to be notable for more than its moral offensiveness. It has been performed in ignorance of the circumstances surrounding it, and the rest of the play represents a kind of atonement worked out by the victim of the pollution. Again, we see the importance of understanding the link between ἁμαρτία as the mistake in identity, and ἀναγνώρισις as the recovery from that mistake. Even at the fringes of the kind of exposition of the text offered by modern scholarship, we can feel something of the enormous differences between modern and the neo-classical conceptions of what Aristotle was talking about. Certainly we have seen enough to be able to say that, while Addison's version appears perfectly acceptable as a neo-classical sentiment about the concerns of tragedy, it fails to take account of the tight framework of organisation within which the *Poetics* was written.

Our examination of Addison's views may conclude with a brief examination of *Spectator*, no. 548 (28 November 1717). In this paper Addison uses the anonymity available to a correspondent to comment that, while *Spectator*, no. 40, had contained only one paragraph devoted to the doctrine of poetic justice, even this had been "controverted by some eminent Criticks" (IV, 462). The poet, he continues, "May still find out some prevailing Passion or Indescretion in his [hero's] Character, and shew it in such a manner, as will sufficiently acquit the Gods of any Injustice in his Sufferings" (IV, 464). Clearly Addison has found it necessary to become more orthodox, but he has become more academic as well. In fact he becomes considerably entangled in the *Poetics* in the course of reworking his position. He argues, for instance, that:

> if in one Place [Aristotle] says that an absolutely Virtuous Man should not be represented as unhappy, this does not justifie any one who shall think fit to bring in an absolutely virtuous Man upon the Stage. Those who are acquainted with that Author's way of writing know very well, that to take the whole Extent of his Subject into his Divisions of it, he often makes use of such cases as are imaginary, and not reducible to Practice: He himself declares that such Tragedies as ended unhappily bore away the Prize in Theatrical Contentions, from those which ended happily.
> (IV, 465)

This last assertion is a repetition of the mistaken idea in no. 40. In reality Aristotle argues for a correlation between "unhappy" and "unpopular" plays, when he defends Euripides from detraction (see 13.53a22-30). Furthermore, the argument that Addison uses to arrive at this mistaken notion is in itself dubious. Though Aristotle does say that a virtuous man should not be represented as unhappy, he does not imply that if you produce one, you should make him happy. (Unhappy endings "pleased the People, and carried away the Prize in the Publick Disputes of the stage"; I. 169).

There is one place where Aristotle says that the worst mode of handling dire incidents is where one person intends to attack another, knowing his identity, and then holds back (14.53b37-8). With some ingenuity one could argue that in this case a good man is virtuous and stays happy. But it is implausible to suggest that Addison had this instance in mind, and in any case the awkward case is presented, not as "imaginary" but because the *Antigone* actually does work like this. Haemon draws his sword upon Creon, and then does not use it on him: he falls upon it himself. Aristotle loved making divisions, this cannot be denied; but it is almost always the case in the *Poetics* that his schemata are accompanied by examples. Addison, then, is open to the charge we made against Dryden. He implies a far greater familiarity with the text than is justified, and he habitually writes with a deceptive confidence that must in many cases have secured him from detection.

It seems particularly true of the debate on poetic justice that the critical temper of the English neo-classical critic determined his interpretation of Aristotle. There were of course two main sources for the doctrine: the text itself and the compulsion to moralise. But one feels that the motivation to read the text as a moralistic document must have been prior to the consultation of it. There is just not enough in the words themselves to support the doctrine, unless one is predisposed to believe that they will support it. It is true that Aristotle says little about ἁμαρτία--it is not actually perverse to give it a moralistic sense. But on the other hand, he is explicit on the question of alternative endings. We must conclude, then, that while the neo-classical elaboration of Aristotle's relatively simple series of statements on the character of the hero and on endings was the life-blood of much neo-classical criticism, the role of the text of the *Poetics* was essentially honorific.

CHAPTER FIVE: CHARLES GILDON

The Complete Art of Poetry (1718) is an amateur's guide to the main doctrines of neo-classicism and to the critics upon whom the canon was founded. Gildon makes acknowledgement of Aristotle ("chiefly"), Horace, Dionysius (though not of Plato or Longinus), and of Boileau, Rapin, Dacier, Vossius, Rymer, and Dennis. He does not acknowledge Dryden or Addison in this list, but they too have some part to play in his work. Of these sources, Dacier, this time in English form, is the most influential, or rather the most used--Gildon's borrowings are too direct and his own comment too infrequent for us to call it "influence". Dacier provides Gildon with his closest contact with the *Poetics*, there being no evidence that he had any first-hand acquaintance with the text in any Greek edition.

It was an article by F.E. Litz in 1942 that first made clear how extensively Gildon's work was derived from the work of others.[1] Litz showed that Gildon's borrowings were very often verbatim and that nearly half were unacknowledged. To his findings we may add that even when Gildon does acknowledge his source as being a commentator on Aristotle, it does not mean that he has made any distinction between what he finds in that commentator and what belongs more immediately to the text of the *Poetics*. The sort of device Gildon used to cover his tracks is well illustrated in the first of his collection of dialogues, where he turns his attention to the origin of poetry and to chapter IV of the *Poetics*. Although Aristotle is only the ultimate source for what Gildon says, Gildon does his best to make it look as though the *Poetics* is his immediate source: "We must take a short View of the first Rise, or Causes of this divine Art among Men; and this I shall borrow from *Aristotle*, the Father and best of *Criticks*".[2]

---

[1] F.E. Litz, "The Source of Charles Gildon's *Complete Art of Poetry*", *ELH*, IX (1942), 118-35.

[2] All references to *The Complete Art of Poetry* (2 vols, London, 1718). The above reference is to I, 34.

Now, not only does Gildon lift what he says subsequently from Dacier's remarks on chapter IV,[3] interspersing comment with snatches of the text, but when he comes to 4.48b10-11 ("The things we look on with distaste, we enjoy contemplating in an accurate imitation"), he uses Aristotle's experiential "we" (ὁρῶμεν, χαίρομεν) as though voicing the opinion of the characters in his dialogue. It would, then, have been possible for Gildon to get away with a good deal of plagiarising and to leave his readers thinking he was being original. One might hesitate to attribute any dubious motives to his practice, and say instead that it suited well with the casually conversational tone of his writing and the fluency of the dialogue form of criticism.

Extending our range a little, and taking account of the level at which Gildon's writing is pitched, we would add that it seems to cater for Addison's old audience, for whom precision in quotation would not be very material. It would thus be better to charge Gildon with being over-ambitious than to accuse him of guile. For though part of his stated aim was to remove "the Ignorance of our Writers ... of *Poesy*" (Preface, p. [a5r.]), there is little in what he says that would benefit the aspiring, or the already wrong-headed, poet. It would have been much more to their advantage to study the originals from which Gildon wrote.

Rymer incorporated Aristotle into his own idiosyncratic criticism, and Dryden made typically judicious use of the *Poetics*; but Gildon has no independence of the kind to be found in them and, in view of his stated aim, not much discrimination either. He is led almost entirely by his sources, and whatever insights on the *Poetics* there may be in his work, they are not generally of his own finding.

The first point of detail that I wish to present will illustrate this. It is plain in the text of chapter IV that Aristotle believes there are two causes (48b4-5) for the origin of poetry. It has, however, long been disputed which of two

---

[3] Litz began his list of borrowings from Dacier too late: Gildon, I, 84-6 represents Dacier's translation IV, i-ii and his remarks IV, 3, 5.

possibilities should be taken to represent the second cause. That the first cause is the naturalness of imitation to man is not disputed: Aristotle says there are "two causes for the origin of poetry, both innate. For imitation is natural to men from childhood up" (48b4-6). However, the problem then arises of whether the pleasure men take in imitation (b8-9), or the naturalness of harmony and rhythm (b20-21), should be regarded as the second cause. The difficulty is increased by the fact that eleven lines of digression and explanation separate the first from the second alternative.

Some say that the first alternative is enough in itself to stand as a cause. They also claim that if the second alternative constitutes the second cause, the amount of explanation attaching to the first cause and the first alternative is hopelessly disproportionate. As Bywater has it: "One would expect [the second alternative] to be brought in in a less incidental way, and with a reason of some sort to justify the position ascribed to [it]", if it were really the second cause (p.127). But when one considers Aristotle's loose and jumbled method of writing, together with the fact that the *Poetics* has long been regarded as a set of notes for lecturing to an esoteric body, then the question of disproportion becomes less material. The kind of argument that Dacier used to defend the position contrary to Bywater's should not be silenced on the mere grounds of awkward presentation.

One might well expect some sort of reason to justify assigning the second cause of poetry to the naturalness of harmony and rhythm to man, but Aristotle can be said to have given one in the very statement that harmony and rhythm are natural. The words κατὰ φύσιν, that introduce the second alternative, can be taken as a deliberate (and resumptive) echo of αἰτίαι ... καὶ αὗται φυσικαί, "two causes, and those innate". Furthermore, as Dacier remarks and Gildon repeats after him, "whatever Inclination Men may have to *Imitation*, yet had that never given Rise to Poetry, if they had not been as much inclin'd to *Number* and *Harmony*" (Gildon, I, 86; Dacier, *Remarks*, IV, 9).

Dacier's point is shrewd. The first cause and the first alternative are adequate to explain the appeal of art as a whole (art being essentially imitative in the *Poetics*): but until one arrives at the second alternative there is no differential to distinguish poetry from all the other arts. The fact that the mention of harmony and rhythm can be made to refer specifically to poetry is not troublesome, for Aristotle makes an aside which remarks that μέτρα ("verses" rather than "verse") are clearly part of rhythm (48b20). Now Dacier does not go to these lengths to explain his assertion, but what we have taken as the critical deciding point (the inclusion of the differential of poetry) is, I think, contained in it. A good piece of interpretation thus finds its way into Gildon, but it is to be doubted whether Gildon would have found it by himself, and typical of him that he offers no additional comment of his own on a disputed matter of some importance.

Gildon produces arguments on the subject of Aristotle's status much akin to those we found in Dennis. Aristotle is the only alternative to chaos in criticism. In accordance with the form of his work Gildon presents both sides of the case. But his spokesman for the moderns (prejudicially named, "Trifle") has only the gaiety and gallantry of modern writing to oppose to the "regular, stiff *Pieces of the Ancients*" (I, 105). "Trifle" is no more than an *advocatus diaboli*, and not a very convincing one at that; for Gildon soon takes to a rather confident hectoring of the moderns. He asserts that the *Spectator* and the *Guardian* "have proceeded no farther than Words, and the subservient Parts of Poetry, but never durst advance to the Disposition of the Parts, and an Oeconomy of an entire Poem" (I, 130). Gildon also noted Dryden's attempt to disturb the traditional order of parts in drama, but himself felt confident in the strength of the traditional position. Furthermore the special circumstances in which Dryden wrote also help Gildon's case. He remarks that "*Criticism*, I mean just *Criticism*, was not [Dryden's] Talent, especially in the Drama; for ... he contradicts himself in his Prefaces, which is a proof that he was by no means fix'd in his judgment" of the place that should be given to diction in the order of parts (I, 225).

We would not concede Gildon the principle that Dryden should not be allowed to change his mind, but we would be willing to recognise that Dryden's emphasis on diction, which constituted his challenge to the traditional order of parts, was perhaps special pleading in favour of heroic drama. Such an emphasis was no longer necessary, when, as in Gildon's time, heroic drama had gone out of favour. Even so, Dryden's attitude to plot would have been given little countenance either. Aristotle's recommendation is reinforced by the lines from the *Essay on Poetry* (1682), where Buckingham is explained to mean, when he says "first on a Plot employ thy careful Thought" (I, 229), that plot comes first not only *quoad fundamentum*, but also *quoad dignitatem*. The acceptability of Aristotle's order was likely to continue while discussion of drama remained in compartments. Even if the traditional order did not do justice to the demands of English drama, it was still possible to give the Manners full scope within those sections of one's criticism devoted to that element. But a new conception of the processes of literary creation and a new attitude to the function and value of poetry was going to be needed before Aristotle's order could be overturned.

Gildon is orthodox in his conception of the function of plot, as well in his view of its status. On this topic we find one of his rare additions to what he found in Dacier. His modifications were generally made to improve phrasing and style, but on the allegorical nature of the fable he finds occasion to add to his authority. He is moved to do so by an opposition to those who advocated literalness in the plot of a play, in order that the audience might believe in it. The poet,

> has the same Right to this Name, when he presents us with true *Incidents*, provided that these true *Incidents* have the Poetic Qualities of Verisimilitude, and that Possibility which is requir'd by the Art. (I, 236)

The concession to the strictly "historical" poet is forced upon him by Aristotle through the medium of Dacier. But it is open to objections, implicit in the preference of poetry over history and the principle that prefers the probable impossibility to the incredible possible (25.61b11-12), and is qualified by Gildon accordingly. He emphasises that verisimilitude and possibility in "true" incidents "are very rare; and therefore a Fable wholly fictitious will generally be more Poetic, as well as more easily adapted to Nature and Art, than any that History does afford" (ibid.).

Since the *Poetics* can be made to support both those who prefer fictitious and those who demand true incidents in their plots, we must pause for a moment to examine the evidence. The key passage is that in which Aristotle defines the universal of poetry. He says that it is "the sort of thing such and such a person happens to say or do, according to likelihood or necessity" (9.51b58-9). Aristotle adds in the same sentence that this is what poetry aims at "giving (ἐπιτιθημένη) names to the characters". For Gildon this has to mean "ev'n while it imposes true Names on the Persons it introduces" (I, 235)--he has to give the participle a concessive force, so that the literal truth of a fable remains subsidiary to its "allegorical and universal" truth. Those, however, who thought literal truth sufficient and desirable, followed an old tradition of commentary that considered, in the words of Robortello, that "if the tragic fable contains an action that ... is not true ... it may perhaps move the minds of the hearers, but certainly less effectively".

These critics had to regard the participle as being causal ("the general is what such and such a person happens to do ... which poetry aims at by giving true names to the characters"). This divergence of interpretation continued: Butcher translated the passage as follows: "it is this universality at which poetry aims in the names she attaches to the personages" (p. 35), and Bywater said that the universal is "the aim of poetry, though it affixes proper names to the characters" (p. 27). Now both interpretations have to make it material that the names the poet gives are known. It is also to be recognised that Aristotle does say (51b15 ff.) that the tragedians adhere to the names they find, because the possible is persuasive, and what has happened ("true incidents") is clearly possible. But he adds immediately afterwards that some tragedies make use of fictitious names and that it would be ludicrous to adhere to known names all the time. He points out that "even the known is known to but a few, and yet pleases all".

The question whether the names are known or not is therefore immaterial: the important principle for Aristotle is that the poet must give his story its general line, *before* he fills out the episodes and adds the names (see 17.55b12-13). Thus once again the *Poetics* is at the mercy of the critical scheme into which it is to be fitted.

It is often stated that the *Poetics* is a seminal work, but, when it comes to detailed citation in the neo-classical age, it sometimes seems that it is auxilliary rather than seminal. It is, then, as an account of the doctrines of neo-classicism based on Aristotle, that *The Complete Art of Poetry* is comprehensive and competent. The question of representation passes from Gildon to Dacier, except where Gildon chooses to pass Dacier off for Aristotle. But even then we have to recognise that the English critics habitually made no distinction between the *Poetics* and commentary upon it. The interpretation of Aristotle acceptable to their age had been made and there was, in the seventeenth and eighteenth centuries, nothing of our modern conception of the nature and function of an edition. We presuppose, for instance, that a modern editor will begin with an accurate historical perspective of the work in hand and a keen appreciation of the intellectual climate of the times at which it was written. The neo-classical critics (at least until the advent of Bentley) did not think along such lines, if only because they ran counter to the principle that the valuable things in Aristotle were true for all ages.

Being, therefore, of necessity true for them, they had no cause to stop and consider whether or not what they saw in Aristotle would have been true for him. If one of Aristotle's commentators says that such and such a thing is the case, it is the same for them as if Aristotle had said it himself. Gildon found supplied to him, once he had made the assumption that Dacier and Aristotle were the same thing, nearly half of what he wrote in a work of some hundred thousand words. He had only the hack-work to do.

CHAPTER SIX: JOSEPH TRAPP

In his capacity as first Professor of Poetry at Oxford, Joseph Trapp delivered in Latin a course of thirty-one lectures on poetry. These were published between 1711 and 1719 under the title of *Praelectiones Poeticae*; but sometime after the issue of his translation of Virgil (1731) which contained notes and essays, some of them complementary to the lectures, it was decided to translate them. They cover the full range of purely theoretic criticism in Trapp's time: in addition to examinations of poetry, of drama in general, of epic, tragedy, and comedy, the work contains coverage of the minor genres, of style, and of sublimity. Aristotle is thus germane to roughly half the work, and of course looms large in those contexts to which he is relevant. Trapp, like Gildon, relies on other people's commentary, but shows more willingness to offer comment.

If we turn to his Author's Preface to the translation, we can place him on his own terms. He contends there that

> every Man, after he has weigh'd the Opinion of others should be at Liberty to follow his own. This method I take to be the most entertaining and the most useful both to the writer and the Reader. No one, I am persuaded, will suspect I pursued it for the sake of Ease; since it is much harder to *digest* than to transcribe.[1]

Trapp thus advertises an intention to follow his own line of interpretation on the important critical questions and we might feel justified in expecting him to look more closely than his predecessors at the text of the *Poetics*. As the convention of his time dictates, Trapp begins his discussion of poetry with a definition of it. It is, in his opinion

---

[1] *Lectures on Poetry* (London, 1742), p. iii. All references are to this version.

> an Art of imitating ... every Being in Nature, and every Object of the Imagination, for the Delight and Improvement of Mankind" (p.13).

Were there any new departures in Trapp, we could expect that "every Being in Nature" indicated a new interest in the natural world, and that "every Object of the Imagination" heralded a concern with the psychological workings of poetry. But Trapp is neither a prophet for James Thomson, nor a disciple of Hobbes,[2] and his criticism looks back to problems that had exercised the Italians two centuries before. Indeed, his discussion is scarcely under way, when he deals with two problems related directly to the *Poetics* about which the Italians had had protracted debate. The problems may be stated as follows: (1) Must the subject of poetry be confined to actions alone? (2) Is verse essential to the medium? Trapp does not draw on Italian commentary in his discussion, he refers to later critics and directly to the text of the *Poetics*. He begins thus:

> is it not the Business of Poetry to represent every Thing that is capable of being represented? And are Actions the only Things capable of being represented? This, indeed, is expressly asserted by *Dacier*, the *French* Interpreter of *Aristotle* [chap. 2, Remarks 1]. But to any one that considers this Passage, it will abundantly appear, that this Opinion cannot be drawn from *Aristotle* by a just Interpretation of him. That great Philosopher, and Prince of Critics, says, that *Imitators imitate Actions*. Now, can any one, without violating all the rules of Reasoning this Philosopher has taught, conclude form hence that Actions *alone* are capable of being imitated? He indeed says [chap. 2, ad init.], that *ALL that imitate, imitate*

---

[2] For possible sources in Aristotle for Hobbes's views of poetry, see C.D. Thorpe, *The Aesthetic Theory of Thomas Hobbes* (Ann Arbor, 1940), p. 129 ff.

Actions; but in his own Original he says no such Thing; the word ALL is added by the Interpreter: His Words are μιμοῦνται οἱ μιμούμενοι πράττοντας, i.e. *Imitators imitate Actions*. [Aristotle] tells us himself, a little before the Passage above cited, μιμοῦνται καὶ ἤθη καὶ πάθη καὶ πράξεις, [1.47a28] i.e. *they imitate Manners, Passions, and Actions*. He thought therefore that not only Actions, but Manners and Affections, were capable of being imitated.   (pp. 13-14)

One notices in this passage some methodological differences that separate Trapp from the other critics with whom we have dealt. Aristotle is not incidental to Trapp's larger purposes, as he generally was for Rymer, Dennis and Dryden, and a greater degree of involvement with the text is thus natural to his critical method. Trapp also differs from Gildon in clearly distinguishing between text and commentary, and in actually inciting his readers to consult the original.

Clearly Trapp is arguing for some extension of Aristotle, but it is restricted to "Manners and Affections"--in other words, here is a further neo-classical attempt to disturb Aristotle's ordering of the qualitative parts of tragedy. Trapp has been very positive, and has quoted the Greek to support his case. But an examination of the context of the passages he quotes tells strongly against him. Since Trapp's whole argument is based on the possibility of imitators imitating things other than actions, his point about logic must be taken. None the less, as regards the contents of the *Poetics*, Trapp is much astray. By the time that the phrase μιμοῦνται οἱ μιμούμενοι πράττοντας appears (2.49al), Aristotle is passing from the medium of imitation in the various arts to the subject of imitation. It is here stated that "since imitators do imitate men in action ... they imitate people either better or worse or the same as us".

Here *expressum facit cessare tacitum*: the *Poetics* states too often that tragedy is an imitation of an action, to make it other than obtuse to suggest that tragedy imitates other things as well. Furthermore, while the subject of both Trapp's quotation is "imitators", his argument requires the term to apply specifically to poets--he is talking about "the Business of Poetry". Now, Trapp has it supplied to him by the Greek that οἱ μιμούμενοι ("imitators") imitate actions, and for both Trapp and Aristotle the word does signify, more immediately, poets. But when he produces the Greek to show that "they" imitate Manners and Passions and Affections, it is concealed from view that in the *Poetics* "they" are "those people", i.e., dancers. Aristotle says that "the art of the dancers uses rhythm, without harmony (for they too imitate characters, and experiences, and actions)" (1,47a26-8). The weight of almost the whole of the *Poetics* tells against any attempt to transfer this assertion from the art of dancing to that of tragedy.

It was a corruption in the text of chapter I that caused Trapp's second problem. Right from its rediscovery, the text had posed a difficulty by making it appear that metre was not essential to poetry, by seeming to suggest that epic had a far larger extension that its usual application to Homer. Trapp begins his discussion of this inherited problem by stating a strong preference: "there may be Verses without a Poem, there can't be a Poem without Verses" (p.19). His intention is not to scorn minor and amateur poets (as the first half of the sentence suggests), but to debar Romance from the dignity of being called poetry (as the second half leaves him room to argue).

The crux comes at 1.47a26 ff., which appears to suggest that epic used either verse or prose in its imitations. In view of the complexities involved, I shall begin by presenting a schematised version of the text on the modern acceptation of it. Aristotle places poetry among the imitative arts at the beginning of the *Poetics*, categorising these arts according to the differences between them in medium, object, and method of imitation. The media of the arts are distinguished in relation to the combinations they use of rhythm, speech, and harmony. Our present crux comes at the conclusion of a long sentence that details which arts use which combinations. Here is the whole sentence:

> Just as some imitate many things through colour and figure (some through technique, others through native skill), and others imitate by the

voice, so the arts we have spoken of make their imitation by rhythm, speech, and melody, and with these either used separately, or mixed together: (a) the flute and the lyre using melody and rhythm alone..., (b) the art of the dancers using rhythm alone, without melody..., (c) the art using only bare prose or verses, and either mixing the verses together or using one kind of metre only, being unnamed up to this time.

Here we have a text that reads, in section (c), ἡ δὲ [μιμητικὴ τέχνη] and ἀνώνυμος τυγχάνουσα. The neo-classicists and their Italian forebears read ἡ δὲ ἐποποιία ... τυγχάνουσα. Where we say that it is a "nameless" art that uses verse or prose, the neo-classicists were told by their text that it was "epic" that did so. The changes made to the text by Ueberweg and Bernays (which have since been substantiated by the Arabic version of the *Poetics*) are such that they do not disturb the syntax of the passage at all and do not affect its sense, except of course in section (c).

It can be seen, then, that though the changes are now universally accepted, there is nothing in the style or the syntax of the section to suggest what they should be, nothing to suggest it is corrupt. Liberally translated, the section would have read "the arts we have spoken of make their imitation by rhythm, speech, and harmony ... the epic happening to be (sc. content with) prose or verse ... up to this time".

There were, then, no pressures on the neo-classicists to change the reading, merely the necessity of explaining its unexpected sense: the labours of German classical philology were needed before the changes were made, neo-classical scholarship being limited in the main to offering changes of a more obvious kind. Dacier, for instance, proposed in his Chapter 18, Remark 16, that at 17.55b17 the text should read οὐ μακρός, not μακρός; it should say that the summary of the *Odyssey* was *not* lengthy. Now the support for the change is plain on the page: Aristotle gives a summary of *Iphigenia Taurica* that occupies six lines, and one of the *Odyssey* that occupies only seven. Common sense therefore suggests something is amiss, and Dacier proposed his emendation accordingly.

With emendation beyond their range, what was it open to the neo-classicists to do with this section of Chapter I? Trapp takes Dacier and Vossius as being representative interpreters in the matter. Those who agree with Dacier, says Trapp, "think they are supported by no less Authority than *Aristotle*'s [in arguing that poetry does not need metre]; who asserts τ' ἐποποιίαν [sic] to consist μόνον τοῖς λόγοις ψιλοῖς, ἢ τοῖς μέτροις". Accordingly, the belief arose that "*Aristotle* admitted some sort of Epic Poem without Metre" into the literature that may be classed as poetry (Trapp, p. 20; cf. Dacier, *Remarks*, I, 22; p. 11). Others, Trapp thinks, would agree with Vossius,³ who defends the opinion that "by λόγοις ψιλοῖς is to be understood poetical Discourse, not without Metre, but with Harmony and Rhythm ... So that ... the Particle ἢ is not disjunctive in this Place, but explanatory" (ibid.).

Which interpretation makes the better use of the evidence available? Let us begin with Vossius. If Aristotle had intended what Vossius thought, then section (c) of the passage above would have been rendered into English as follows:

> epic uses poetical discourse without harmony
> and rhythm, but not without metre, and mixes
> the metres or uses them singly (as it has done)
> up to the present time.

But it would then be necessary to come to terms with the explanatory sentence that follows:

> For we have no common term to use of mime,
> τοὺς Σωκρατικοὺς λόγους, and imitations in
> various metres.

---

³ Trapp refers to the *De Artis Poeticae Natura ac Constitutione* (Amsterdam, 1647), pp. 7-8.

The words τοὺς Σωκρατικοὺς λόγους, on this interpretation, were in fact made to apply to the metric versions of Aesop that Socrates made when in prison (see *Phaedo*, 61a-b; cf. Dacier, *Remarks*, I, 28; p. 12). But to maintain that Aristotle extended the term ἐποποιία is one thing; to suggest that he also narrowed the sense of τοὺς Σωκρατικοὺς λόγους so that they no longer signified the Socratic dialogues, is another. The idea that Socrates' latter-day effort could be regarded by Aristotle as a separate literary form is not credible. Vossius's interpretation must fall on this account.

    The rival interpretation does not have to resort to quite such unlikely devices to explain the passage. Taking ψιλοῖς λόγοις to mean prose, its supporters then have to explain what Aristotle could have had in mind as prose-poetry. But they have the Socratic dialogues readily to hand as an example. Furthermore, there are passages in the *Symposium* and in the *Phaedrus* that could answer well to this description. The motivation behind the alternative interpretations, as far as the neo-classical critics are immediately concerned with the literary theory of their day, is the desire either to include or to exclude Romance from the dignity of being called poetry. Trapp himself modifies his original statement, that there can be no poem without verse, by allowing that ψιλοῖς λόγοις probably does mean "prose". He does, however, still debar such literary forms as the Spanish romance from inclusion under the title of "epic": it is only "the *Novel* or Fable in Prose" that is to be given countenance.

    His account is at fault, in that he gives no examples of what this literary form is, or might be, in practice. He excludes Lucian and Heliodorus among the ancients, but does not say whether or not the Socratic dialogues, for instance, may be called "novels". However, perhaps a lucky accident gained him some support among those of his readers who did not know Latin. The translation of the *Praelectiones Poeticae* appeared in the same year as *Joseph Andrews* (1742). If they had read Fielding's Preface, Trapp's readers might well have favoured his view that the novel should be considered as a form of epic, since Fielding argued for the literary status of his new species of writing on the grounds that it was a comic epic-poem in prose. Fielding himself did not make any reference to the passage we have had under consideration, but the argument he does use to locate his new form of writing is usefully complementary to its preferable interpretation.

Fielding argues that epic is to be divided, like drama, into the serious and the comic, and he points out that Homer wrote in both veins. He then divides poetry into that written in metre and that written in prose. Finally, he ranks the *Telemachus* with Homer's *Odyssey* rather than with "those voluminous works commonly called Romances, namely, Clelia, Cleopatra, [and] the Grand Cyrus".

After the early lectures on poetry, Trapp takes an excursion into the minor genres, to which Aristotle is irrelevant. Not until the subject of drama comes up for consideration does the *Poetics* again become germane to his discussion. Then, when Trapp makes his attempt to place Tragedy (in relation, of course, to epic), Aristotle's preference presents him with a difficulty which many critics in his age preferred to ignore. There was a strong party, led by Rapin and Le Bossu, that considered epic to be beyond dispute the finer and nobler form. Trapp, as a Virgilian, shares this opinion, but he feels it also necessary to relate his preference to what the *Poetics* says on the matter. He writes that:

> *Aristotle*, in the last Chapter of his Book of Poetry, does not scruple to give the Preference to Tragedy before Epic. Not that I think he reckons it a more noble Kind in *general*, (for that would be contrary to Truth and Reason) but only so far as its Sphere extends: And this is a Difference which, I humbly conceive, is very distinguishable.
>
> (p. 238)

I understand Trapp to mean here that tragedy, to the extent that it may be compared with epic (there being large areas where they do not overlap), may be said to be superior; but that on the other hand, there are elements in epic not to be found in tragedy. In these areas the dignity of epic admits of no qualification. It is difficult to decide whether or not

Trapp's contention matches with Aristotle's judgment, but I think it can be argued that Aristotle does not confine the boundaries of comparison quite as sharply as Trapp implies. It seems to me that Trapp's argument relies in part on the assumption that epic has elements that tragedy cannot match--there must be something at stake if it is "contrary to Truth and Reason" to assert that tragedy is superior to epic. But there are some indications, at least, that Aristotle would have come near to maintaining that it was.

Aristotle gives his verdict to tragedy in accordance with what for him was the fundamental principle of all art, that of size as it determines form and, ultimately, beauty. Furthermore, he says not only that tragedy contains all the virtues that are to be found in epic, but also that he who knows about tragedy will know about epic (5.49b17). Epic can be simple or complex, moral or pathetic; it can have recognition, peripeteia, and pathos; it has plot, character, thought, and diction (see 24.59b7-11). Finally, in his detailed comparison, Aristotle argues that tragedy has all that epic has (26.62a14), that its immediacy is felt in reading as well as in action (62a17-18), and that it achieves its end in a shorter span (52a18-b1). This last consideration is crucial, because clearly Aristotle recalls his principle of size as it regulates beauty when he says that the compact is more pleasing than that which is diluted by a great length of time (62b1-2). It thus appears to me that both critics recognise an overlap between tragedy and epic, but that Trapp favours dilation, where Aristotle prefers contraction. Trapp himself is not completely happy with the suggestion he made, even though he maintains that its terms are "very distinguishable". He remarks that though the *Poetics* is defective, "the rest of it appears to have been spent on the same Subject" (p. 238). And Trapp resists writing more on Aristotle's behalf in an attempt to put the *Poetics* in line with the common preference of his day.

I do not intend to canvass Trapp's discussion of epic and tragedy in detail. A great deal of what he said was merely the common parlance of his time. The rest of this chapter will deal, therefore, with some few points in which Trapp's independent contribution to doctrine is of interest, and where his handling of the *Poetics* (or ignorance of it) calls for special comment.

Trapp's remarks on tragedy are as consistently indebted to Vossius as Gildon's were to Dacier; with the difference that Trapp uses Vossius's opinions as a point of departure for his own divergent views.[4] Trapp's comments often constitute the kind of philosophical generalising upon the subject in hand that we have already noted in Dennis, Dryden, and Addison. But even so, it comes as something of a surprise to find Trapp concluding his disagreement with Vossius, over the character of the hero in tragedy, with the remark that he is not at all persuaded that the rules Vossius advanced were really Aristotle's--and that Vossius does not tell him where to find them if they are. This leaves one wondering how much attention Trapp gave to Dacier either, and in sympathy with the impatience of Trapp's editors when they point out that the rules's "are very easy to be found in c. [XIII] of Aristotle's Art of Poetry".[5]

Trapp's confession of ignorance makes it doubtful whether he knew more either of the text of the *Poetics*, or of its sense in translation, than he could pick up from the remarks of others. But even granted that he had read the work entire, if he knew so little about the contents of chapter XIII as to be able to admit to doubt on the rules for the tragic hero, then his reading was wasted labour.

The next matter with which we have to deal reinforces the doubts we have just expressed. Trapp makes lengthy quotation from Vossius's *Poeticarum Institutionum* on the subject of endings in tragedy. His own initial position is that it is enough if "Incidents of Distress and Sorrow are carried on thro' the whole" (p. 310). To support his view he quotes further from Aristotle's Greek and mentions that happy endings are thought to be better, but only because

---

[4] Trapp read both the *De Artis Poeticae Natura ac Constitutione* and *Poeticarum Institutionum* (both Amsterdam, 1674), though his interest lies more with the latter work.

[5] The reference of Clarke and Bowyer is to "c.XIV ... according to *Dan. Heinsius*'s Edition, c. XIII in others" (p. 318n.).

they "humour the wrong or weak judgment of an Audience".[6] That Trapp is at bottom unfamiliar with the contents of the text is further indicated by his then charging Vossius with inconsistency in this area. Vossius is thought to be hovering, when he says that while it is not essential for a tragedy to end happily, those that do, borrow something from comedy. Trapp's translators point out that Vossius depends directly upon Aristotle for this assertion. Indeed, the words to support Vossius appear in the sentence immediately after the one Trapp quotes in the Greek.

I have already hinted that there is something of the neo-classical vein of humane speculation in Trapp's account of tragedy. It finds its best outlet in the topic closely allied to the question of endings--the quality of the tragic hero's character. Trapp's remarks on this topic are chiefly notable as a contrast to the sanctimonious attitude adopted by some critics when discussing vice and virtue, rewards and punishments. This self-satisfied tone seems to have its origins in that paragon of public virtue, Cicero. "Who ... is ever mov'd at the Punishment of a Traitor, or a Parricide?" asks Cicero in his public-safety voice. "It should rather raise a Sort of Satisfaction in us, to think that Justice has overtaken those that have so well deserv'd it", echoes Vossius. Trapp, however, will have none of this: "all good and generous Minds are affected with *Compassion* at the Execution of Rebels and Traitors; and nothing can be more *terrible* than the Punishment inflicted upon some of them" (p. 317). An extension of these sentiments into dramatic criticism might have made for a more liberal approach to the handling of character in drama, but it is not forthcoming. Trapp has already found he can "by no means approve of those Tragedies of ours, in which Persons of equal Innocence and Virtue, of the same Rank and Eminence, are punish'd and rewarded promiscuously" (p. 310).

Furthermore, not only does Trapp fail to project his humane feelings into dramatic theory, but his translators counter what little effect they might have had. When Trapp challenges Vossius on the "sort of Satisfaction" that

---

[6] Trapp, p. 313; *Poetics*, 13.53a33-4.

punishment might raise, his translators add a note to the effect that Aristotle felt in exactly the same way. In their attempt to demonstrate this, they append the phrase οὔτε ἐλεεινον οὔτε φοβερὸν ἔσται τὸ συμβαῖνον,[7] "the outcome will be neither pitiable nor fearful", when the wicked man is plunged into misfortune. What they omit to mention is that Aristotle's immediately preceding words contend that this very situation would be sympathetically received; τὸ γὰρ φιλάνθρωπον ἔχοι ἂν (13.53a2-3).

Many neo-classicists seem to have been too ready to assume their superiority to the general run of mankind to have been able to apply Aristotle on the terms he laid down. Eighteenth-century poetry is, after all, far from egalitarian in feeling. Their notions would perhaps be reinforced by the implication of the *Poetics* that pity is reserved for those unlike, but above, ourselves; and it is "equal Rank and Eminence" that Trapp mentions, together with "Innocence and Virtue", in advocating poetic justice. But such impressions, had they existed, would not have been imperilled by any close reading of Aristotle's tight organisation of terms.

We saw in an earlier chapter that Addison designates pitiable as a situation that Aristotle thought morally outrageous. The precise application of the emotional complex pity-and-fear in the *Poetics* is to be understood when--the inter-relation of ἁμαρτία, ἀναγνώρισις and περιπέτεια being fully grasped--κάθαρσις is seen to be operative as the link between the two complexes. General notions of sympathy for one's fellow men have no place within this tight framework.

As with Rymer, it would falsify the position Aristotle occupies in Trapp's criticism to spin a continuous thread out of the material he uses and the attitudes he expresses. There is, of course, a totality in Trapp's lectures, if they are taken as a résumé of neo-classical doctrine; but the *Poetics* contributed so fragmentarily to the canon, and the text was given such cursory and oblique attention, there was no chance of its being seen as a whole, of its appearing in

---

[7] φαίνεται Clarke and Bowyer; ἔσται all MSS.

criticism with any cohesion. Trapp's task involved him in comment and correction to a certain extent, but even he assumes that in the main the acceptable adaptation of Aristotle to his age has been made. While, then, he might, and perhaps ought, to have gained more familiarity with the text than the other critics we have examined, he was in fact content to come only so close to Aristotle as his sources permitted. We ought not to scorn Trapp for operating within the limits of his day, but it was open to him to discover more than he did about the context of the remarks he took direct, we are to suppose, from Aristotle. His actual method leads us to realise just how little direct relation Aristotle's text could have in the critical tradition founded on it. The neo-classical method of exposition forced Aristotle's intended sense into obscurity, his own terms completely into the background, and even the literal sense of his words was thoroughly fragmented.

CHAPTER SEVEN: JAMES HARRIS

Two aspects of the writings of James Harris could have made him one of the most important and interesting critics of his time: he was the first to show some interest in Aristotle's philosophy in an aesthetic context, and the best acquainted with Aristotle's Greek. In the event, however, his productions are something of a disappointment. There is a great deal more gesticulation than action in the style and temper of his criticism--a characteristic one sees reflected in the overly fussy typography of the later eighteenth century. The immediacy and vitality has gone from the study of the *Poetics*, and there is no accession of scholarly acumen and precision to replace it--this was to come eight years later, with Twining's translation and notes.

The fact that Harris is not as significant as his qualifications might have enabled him to be does not mean, however, that he should have been omitted from consideration; rather that we have to work very much by inference in those areas where he is of interest. A judicious use of his writings, particularly the first two and the last,[1] will enable us to make up a deficiency in our view of the *Poetics* in neo-classical criticism. From him we can draw at least some impression of what the late neo-classical conception was of the relation between Aristotle's critical and his philosophical doctrines.

Because the critics with whom we have been concerned so far have shown no interest in Aristotle's philosophy as a guide to the *Poetics*, we have given attention to what they supplied in its place. Harris, however, became very enthusiastic about Aristotle's philosophy, ridding himself of what his son called "a prejudice, very common at that time even among scholars, that Aristotle was an obscure and unprofitable author, whose philosophy had been deservedly superseded by that of Mr. Locke" (I, xii-xiii).

---

[1] "Concerning Art: a Dialogue", "A Discourse on Music, Painting, and Poetry", both first published in *Three Treatises* (1741); and *Philological Inquiries* (1781). All my references are to *The Works of James Harris* (5 vols, London, 1803).

Indeed, the first of his published works contained a general theory of art largely based, as Harris timidly confessed at its conclusion, on Aristotle's four causes. Thinking, then, of the importance of works like Butcher's *Aristotle's Theory of Poetry and Fine Art*, with its examination of the *Poetics* in the larger context of Aristotle's philosophy, we would have welcomed even an isolated neo-classical attempt to interpret the one in the light of the other. But though Harris wrote on the philosophy in his first critical piece, and on the *Poetics* in his second, it seems never to have occurred to him to fuse his two interests together and to allow one topic to complement and illuminate the other.

Thus, for Harris, the two fields are independent, and our hypothetical projection of the philosophy onto the criticism, to be made on Harris's behalf, will tend to reinforce rather than to challenge the traditional view of the *Poetics*.

I wish here to make a résumé of Harris's theory of art based on Aristotle, and to compare his aesthetic with what he and his age thought about the *Poetics*. My account of the theory can be brief, since the latter comprises no more than elementary observations about the principles of Aristotle's philosophy. Harris should not be accused of superficiality, however, when his age had so little taste for, and so little knowledge of, the writings outside the *Poetics* and the *Rhetoric*. But while there is little in Harris's Dialogue that even a passing acquaintance with Aristotle's philosophy would fail to embrace, it is difficult to imagine what Harris thought his readers would have made of his theory. He does not make his acknowledgement to the four causes, once famous among Schoolmen, until right at the end of the *Dialogue* (see I, 44). His presentation, in other words, is to some extent self-stultifying.

It is easy, though, to see what he intended. His method is to present his material in the style and manner of the Socratic dialogues, toning down the substance and thrusting the casually conversational mode to the fore. By this means he hoped his readers would be diverted by the *Dialogue* and subsequently informed by the notes--but they would certainly have received little enlightenment before they turned to them.

First Harris determines the efficient cause of art, which he defines as "an Habitual Power in Man of becoming the Cause of some Effect, according to a system of various and well-approved Precepts" (I, 17). The key word here is "habitual", since the *Rhetoric* (I, 10) has decided Harris's choice. He has found there that Aristotle gives seven possible causes for action in life, and that only one of these has all the qualities necessary for artistic creation.

Three causes (nature, external compulsion, and chance) are dismissed because they preclude choice and the conscious intention of the artist. "Nature", in this case is "natural necessity", the mechanical operation of living creatures. Three more causes are rejected on the grounds that they do not coincide with the mode of operation adopted by the artist. These three causes, designated "natural faculties", cover man's natural endowments, such as sight, but not his acquired faculties. "Custom", however, does cover the area Harris has in mind. The artist has freedom of choice, but he is also dependent, for the exercise of his power, both on his own practice and that of others.

"*Art*", says Harris, "implies not only *Cause*, but the additional Requisite of *Intention*" (I, 7). This must be bolstered by "*Use, Practice,* [and] E*xperience*" (I, 9). To borrow a term from the rhetorical tradition, the *exercitatio* of the artist also operates within the limits that those precepts impose upon him, whose virtue lies in their "*Number* and *Dignity*" (I, 15). Now, though Harris makes no comment on its application to the *Poetics* when making Aristotle's *ethos* the efficient cause of art, it is easy to see where the neo-classical attitude toward the *Poetics* could have been brought in. The identification of "a" system of various and well approved precepts that control the artists activity with "the" system, namely Aristotle's, would surely have been made by any formalist critic who read this passage.

We have already seen more than once that the formalist stood firmly by Aristotle because he thought him the only alternative to chaos. As Dennis said, if Aristotle's are not the rightful rules of poetry, then it is not an art, because there are no other. We may conclude, then, that Harris's age, which saw Aristotle and Reason operating in conjunction with each other, received from Harris a justification for its view drawn by direct extension from Aristotle's philosophy.

Turning next to the material cause of art, Harris determines that the common or universal subject of art is "all those contingent Natures, which lie within the reach of human Powers to influence" (I, 22). The background to Harris's otherwise uninformative statement is supplied this time by the *Physics*. His authority tells him that the aims of nature are such that they may or may not be achieved. Things that are necessary cannot but happen: things impossible cannot happen at all; but between these extremes lies the contingent, to which sphere the world largely belongs. Some things, however, even though subject to frustration, do have a greater tendency to achieve their end than to be thwarted. In the natural world "complete animals are more frequently born than monsters", and in the world of the artist, for example of the musician, the right string is struck more often than the wrong (I. 267).

In thus limiting the artist's domain to what he is humanly able to conceive of and control, Harris permits to Aristotle's definition of the universals of poetry a standing of its own. The "universal" world of the poet is limited by Aristotle to the sort of thing that is done and said by men, just as the universal that man's mind naturally reaches out to comprehend is inherent in the particular objects around him. In this instance, then, Harris may offer something of a check to the more thoroughly neo-classical position that has been adopted by Dacier and Dennis. The poet does not "examine that Universal Nature, which is always perfect" (Hooker, I, 73), because something that is *always* perfect cannot be contingent--it must be necessary. Perhaps, however, we need to be rather careful here in attributing Platonic notions to Dacier and Dennis. We have seen that "nature" is, for them, notional rather than actual, and we might hazard that they would disagree with Dryden for this reason, where he says that "as for a perfect character of virtue, it never was in nature" (I, 246). But even they, at least to the extent that they would not allow a man of perfect virtue into tragedy, would agree that "there can be no imitation of it" (ibid.).

Even the formalist's view of the poet's world does become subject to the limitations of probability: it is one where the persuasive impossibility is to be preferred before the event that has happened, but is difficult to credit. It would have been interesting to see which party found more support from Harris, those who thought that historical plausibility was the essential factor in the plot, or those (Dacier and Dennis among them) who subsumed "historical" truth under the "universal and allegorical" truth of the fable. Unfortunately, however, Harris does not give a version of *Poetics*, 9.51b8-10, he does not say whether the poet aims at the universal *by* imposing names, or *though* imposing names, on his characters.

In the *Dialogue*, poetry is not given separate or specific attention. However, the companion piece, which is entitled "A Discourse on Music, Painting and Poetry", makes detailed comparison of the spheres of the three arts. There Harris lays down for tragedy the special function of eradicating pity and fear, but he does so only in passing, and we may presume that tragedy is not excluded from the judgments made on poetry in relation to the arts of painting and music. Now poetry in general (and, we may assume, tragedy too) is commended by Harris for its ability and special aptitude in dealing with subjects "so framed as to lay open the *internal Constitution of Man*" (I, 84). It gives us "an Insight into *Characters, Manners, Passions*, and *Sentiments*" (ibid.)--a list from which "action" is conspicuously absent. Man, then, as a contingent nature, is the proper study of the poet; and Harris, by his emphasis, joins the ranks of those in the eighteenth century whose natural impulse was to give more importance in drama to character than to plot.

The evidence drawn here from the "Discourse" comes merely by implication, but at the other end of his career, in his last work, Harris was still of the same mind. When dealing extensively with the *Poetics*, Harris stands by Aristotle's order of parts and places plot first. But he recognises at the same time that

> even in the Plays we most admire, we shall seldom find our Admiration to arise from the *Fable*: 'tis either from *the Sentiment*, as in *Measure for Measure*; or from the purity of *the Diction*, as in *Cato*; or from the *Characters* and *Manners*, as in *Lear, Othello, Falstaff,*

> *Benedict* and *Beatrice*, [and] *the School for Scandal*. (IV, 164-5)

Here we can only feel that Harris's theoretical acceptance of Aristotle's preference and emphasis which constitutes his rule, is contradicted by his making some of the best English drama exceptions to that rule. He gives his approval to Lillo's *The Fatal Curiosity*, the play that fits best with the theory he outlines. Lillo's play was not so much a poor choice to illustrate "the *Universality* of the Precepts" Aristotle gives (IV, 142), as an indication that the prominence given to plot and structure (the grounds on which Harris commends *The Fatal Curiosity*) were an embarrassment to English critics. Probably few, even in Harris's day, would allow *The Fatal Curiosity* to stand as England's counterpart to *Oedipus Tyrannus*, merely in order that Aristotle's emphasis on plot might be maintained.

So far we have found some reinforcement in Harris's theory for both the neo-classical view of the subject of poetry and its concept of how poetry should be written: it should deal with the characters of men, and it should conform to a system of rules in which Aristotle and reason coincide. In his rather colourless definition of the formal and final causes of art, Harris also reflects his age. He determines merely that art tends towards the benefit of mankind. He does so, because he is again having to work within limits. The Greek word τέχνη covers both art and craft, and, to conform to his authority, Harris has to produce a definition that will cover the making of clothes as well as the writing of poetry and the painting of pictures. He thus gives to the artist's work an immediate end: the production of the work, and an remoter end: himself and others. Had he narrowed his discussion down to tragedy, Harris would of course have immediately had it open to him to introduce the Horatian requirement that poetry please and instruct. His theory, then, would clearly have toned in with the conceptions of his age.

A more lively writer, a critic with more address, might have taken Harris's occasion to produce something new, but Harris himself merely furthers the withdrawal of Aristotle into academicism in the course of the eighteenth century. In the late seventeenth century and the early part of the eighteenth, Aristotle was part of a lively criticism with practical concerns. By the second decade, however, he was already appearing in contexts that had much less critical urgency than before. Rymer and Dryden took Aristotle to the coffee-house, Addison and Gildon withdrew him to the drawing-room, Trapp and Harris buried him in the study.

Select Bibliography

Addison, Joseph. *The Spectator,* ed. D.F. Bond. 5 vols, Oxford, 1965.

Averroes. "Paraphrasis in Librum Poeticae Aristotelis" in *Aristotelis Opera cum Averrois Commentariis.* Vol. 2. Venice, 1562.

Bray, René. *La Formation de la doctrine classique en France.* Paris, 1961.

Bredvold, L.I. *The Intellectual Milieu of John Dryden*. Ann Arbor, 1914.

Butcher, S.H. *Aristotle's Theory of Poetry and Fine Art.* 4th edn, New York, 1951.

Bywater, Ingram. *Aristotle on the Art of Poetry.* Oxford, 1909.

Clark, A.F.B. *Boileau and the French Classical Critics in England (1660-1830).* Paris, 1926.

Crane, R.S. "The Concept of Plot and the Plot of *Tom Jones*", in *Critics and Criticism.* Chicago, 1952.

Dacier, André. *La Poétique d'Aristote.* Paris, 1692.

Dennis, John. *The Critical Works,* ed. E.N. Hooker. 2 vols, Baltimore, 1939.

Diehls, Hermann. *Die Fragmente der Vorsokratiker*. Berlin, 1922.

Drake, James. *The Ancient and Modern Stages Survey'd.* London, 1699.

Dryden, John. *Of Dramatic Poesy, and Other Critical Essays,* ed. G. Watson. 2 vols, London, 1962.

Dryden and Howard 1564-1668: The Text of "An Essay of Dramatic Poesy", "The Indian Emperor", and "The Duke of Lerma", with Other Controversial Matter, ed. D. Arundel. Cambridge, 1929.

Dutton, G.B. "The French Aristotelian Formalists and Thomas Rymer", *PMLA*, XXIX (1914), 152-88.

Eade, J.C. "British Editions of Aristotle's *Poetics* to 1794", *The Library*, 5th ser., XXX (September 1975), 238-41.

Eliot, T.S. *The Sacred Wood*. London, 1960.

Else, G.F. *Aristotle's Poetics: The Argument.* Cambridge, Mass., 1957.

Gildon, Charles. *The Complete Art of Poetry.* 2 vols, London 1718.

Harris, James. "Concerning Art: a Dialogue", "A Discourse on Music, Painting, and Poetry", both first published in *Three Treatises*. London, 1741.

----. *Philological Inquiries*. London, 1781. (All my references are to *The Works of James Harris*. 5 vols, London, 1803.)

Herrick, M.T. *Aristotle's "Poetics" in England*. New Haven, 1930.

Jones, John. *On Aristotle and Greek Tragedy*. London, 1962.

Le Bossu, Réné. *Traité du poeme epique.* Paris, 1675.

Litz, F.E. "The Sources of Charles Gildon's *Complete Art of Poetry*", *ELH*, IX (1942), 118-35.

Montmollin, D. *La Poétique d'Aristote: Texte primitif et additions ultérieures*. Neuchatel, 1951.

Rapin, Réné, *Réflexions sur la poétique d'Aristote.* Paris, 1674.

Robortello, Francesco. *In librum Aristotelis de arte poetica explicationes.* Florence, 1548.

Rymer, Thomas, *The Critical Works*, ed. C.A. Zimansky. New Haven, 1956.

Saintsbury, George. *A History of Criticism and Literary Taste in Europe.* London, 1900-1904.

Sherwood, Margaret. *Dryden's Dramatic Theory and Practice.* Boston, 1898.

Spingarn, J.E. *Critical Essays of the Seventeenth Century.* 2 vols, Oxford, 1908-1909.

Thorpe, C.D. *The Aesthetic Theory of Thomas Hobbes.* Ann Arbor, 1940.

Trapp, Joseph. *Lectures on Poetry.* London, 1742.

Twining, Thomas. *Aristotle's Treatise of Poetry, Translated.* London, 1789.

Vettori, Pietro. *Commentarii in primum librum Aristotelis de arte poetarum.* Florence, 1560.

Vossius, Isaac. *De Artis Poeticae Natura ac Constitutione.* Amsterdam, 1647.

----. *Poëticarum Institutionum.* Amsterdam, 1674

Welsted, Leonard. "A Dissertation concerning the English Language", Preface to *Epistles, Odes, Etc.* London, 1723.